If I Knew Then 2

Warrior Reflections

Edited by Brian R. Willis

Library and Archives Canada Cataloguing in Publication

If I Knew Then 2: Warrior Reflections/Edited by Brian R. Willis—
First Edition

Issued also in electronic format
ISBN 978-0-9808819-3-6

1. Police training. 2. Police--Attitudes. I. Willis, Brian R.

HV7923.1342 2011   363.2   C2011-900414-3

© 2011 by Brian R. Willis
ISBN 978-0-9808819-3-6 (print)
ISBN 978-0-9808819-4-3 (digital)

All rights reserved. Except for use in a review, no portion of this book may be reproduced in any form without the expressed written permission of the publisher.

Publisher:
Warrior Spirit Books
A Division of Winning Mind Training Inc.
246 Stewart Green S.W., Suite #2486
Calgary, Alberta T3H 3C8 Canada
Visit our website www.warriorspiritbooks.com

Design and Production:
Nadien Cole Advertising, Calgary, Alberta

Project Management: Debbie Elicksen, Freelance Communications, Calgary, Alberta

Cover Photographs: Mike Starchuk

If I Knew Then 2: Warrior Reflections—First Edition

Printed and Bound in United States
Copyright 2011

Table of Contents

Foreword by Charles Remsberg 9

Introduction 13

Escape From Evanescence (The Trainer's Creed) 15

Am I That Man? by Ron Scheidt 17

Crafting a Positive Culture of Training
by Timothy Patton 21

The Critics by Jim Niemen 29

Developing Expertise While Maintaining
the Work-life Balance by Chris Lawrence 35

Don't Treat Your Kids Like Suspects
by Leonard Dafoe 43

Everyone is a Leader by Brian Willis 49

For The Right Reasons by Ed Nowicki 55

It's Not About Me by Brian Willis 61

Learning Not to be Selfish by David McRoberts 67

Life is a Precious Gift by Vince O'Neill 73

Nothing is Forever by Guy Rossi 81

On Weakness and Strength by Jack Colwell 85

Reader Writer Thinker Fighter: The Way
of Ronin by Bill Westfall 89

Regaining Perspective by Guy Rossi 103

Riding for the Brand by Roger Higby 107

Seek Ethical Associates and Mentors
by Todd Fletcher 115

Social Intelligence Isn't for Sissies by Chris Bratton 119

Start Mapping Your Career Path Now!
by Bruce Sokolove 125

Take All Training Seriously. Live The Tactical
Lifestyle! by Steven Mosley 133

The Four Ranges of a Fight by Kelly Keith 139

The Power of Questions by Brian Willis 145

The Struggle Within by Harvey Hedden 151

The Warrior's Path by Chip Huth 157

Things They Don't Tell You in the Academy
by James Dowle 163

Where Your Treasure Is, There Your Heart
Will Be Also by Travis Yates 171

The Witch Hunt by Guy Rossi 177

Would I Have by Tim Harder 181

Your Life IS Your Legacy by Brian Willis 187

Acknowledgements

Putting together a book like this takes a great deal of work from a number of people and I would be remiss if I did not thank those people.

I need to start by thanking my wife Lynda. For the past 30 years as the wife of a cop and now a professional speaker and trainer she has put up with shift work, long hours at work, my being away from home, as well as my injuries, excuses, idiosyncrasies, and my long hours on the computer. Through it all she has been loving, encouraging, understanding and supportive.

My two sons Jesse and Cody continue to serve as sounding boards, coaches, mentors and inspiration for me. Their wisdom, insights and ability to cut to the core of an issue both inspires me and fills me with pride. They make it fun to be a dad.

My parents, Bob and Terry, are two of the best role models a person could ever have. Their unconditional love and support along with their selflessness and love for life are truly an inspiration.

While my name goes on the front cover of the book, my role in this project is in many ways the easiest. I simply reached out to law enforcement professionals and asked them three questions.

1. What is one thing you know now that you wish you knew at the start of your career?

2. What is one piece of advice you would give to someone starting out in the profession?
3. Are you willing to write a submission for If I Knew Then 2?

When they said yes, I simply provided some gentle reminders of deadlines and served as the central clearing house for all the submissions. Each of the people who contributed to this book made time in their already hectic lives to share their stories and experiences so that all of us could benefit from their years of experience. I know they spent hours writing, rewriting, editing, tweaking and rewriting their submissions. The fact they asked for nothing in return speaks volumes about their character. I am very grateful for their sacrifice and commitment.

As with the first book *If I Knew Then: Life Lessons From Cops on the Street* I was honored by the contributions of my editorial team. This great team consists of Associate Editor Andrew Prince, my older brother Jim Willis and my brother-in-law Ian McRobbie. Like the professionals who wrote for this book they spent countless hours reading, rereading and editing every submission. They fit this into their busy lives and asked nothing in return for their efforts. They put in countless hours carefully reviewing and editing every submission. Their professionalism, support and understanding of my goals and timelines for this project are greatly appreciated.

Mike Starchuk of Mike Starchuk Photography (http://mikestphoto.com) once again stepped up to do the front cover of the book. This is the fourth book cover Mike has done for Warrior Spirit Books and as always he did an amazing job. Mike has been a mentor, sounding board, and friend to me since we started working together in 1995.

I also need to thank Colin Chisholm for working with Mike as the model for the cover. In addition to being an excellent model Colin is a great father, husband, brother in law and a great cop.

Debbie Elicksen (Canada's Publishing Expert™) from Freelance Communications and Nadien Cole from Nadien Cole Advertising take all the submissions and work their magic to turn out a great finished product.

Thank you for purchasing this book and helping to support our continuing contributions to the ILEETA Fellowship Fund.

Take care.

Brian Willis

Foreword

Face-in-the-mirror introspection is a tough activity, because done honestly it usually involves admissions that can be painful.

You may have to acknowledge that you did not always know as much about life and the world as you probably thought you did. You may have to own up to mistakes that hurt yourself or others. And you may have to face the fact that you're still living with misjudgments of the past—and probably always will. Most people don't wish they could change what they've done unless they've paid a price for it.

In volume two of his powerful series *If I Knew Then*, Brian Willis has once again asked premier law enforcement figures in North America to reflect candidly on the lessons they've learned from their years behind the badge. He requested from each contributor just one bit of hard-won knowledge that they wish they'd known when they started on the job. Being dedicated warriors, they didn't settle for easy platitudes. They selflessly opened up a vein and let unvarnished truths flow out. And few stopped with just one gemstone of advice.

From the voices of experience captured in these pages, you'll hear street veterans talk candidly about stumbles they've made professionally and personally and insights they've gained along the way. The tactics and techniques of arrest and control are not what dominate their observations. When they "shut their eyes in order to see," as the artist Paul Gauguin once described contemplative reflection, what emerge are lessons of survival rarely discussed in police circles.

For example, Travis Yates notes that "There will come a time in your life when being a police officer is not the center of your entire world…. The only thing that lasts in your life is your family." In that regard, he writes poignantly, "I missed a lot of years." He offers seven rules of financial management that he himself ignored because of misguided priorities that haunt him still. "If I only knew then what I know now, the thoughts in my head would be so much more peaceful."

Chris Bratton cites the "long time" it took him to "figure out that social intelligence [is] a critical survival skill in this business…. Little did I guess that it was the stuff that makes and breaks careers and lives."

With touches of mocking humor, Leonard Dafoe refers to the "retroactive wisdom" he gained after treating his own daughter "like a suspect" while channeling his paternal energy into an ill-conceived crusade to nurture juveniles he encountered on the job. "Don't be a cop at home nor a parent at work," he advises.

From his policing experiences as well as from his relationship with a brother who committed murder, David McRoberts says he has learned that selfishness is the driving factor behind most of the moral and judgmental mistakes we make. "If you learn nothing else in life, take any and all steps necessary to avoid becoming a selfish person and the rest of your life just might fall into place more painlessly, with a greater degree of satisfaction and serenity."

Jack Colwell eloquently addresses emotional choices. "Self-righteous indignation will make you feel strong but it brutalizes your soul, destroys your relationships, and renders you devoid of influence…. Humility will make you feel weak but it builds character, nourishes relationships, and releases influence…. With humility you will see the lifestyles and choices of others as a reminder of your own weaknesses and compromises…. With compassion you can accomplish impartial service to the Law rather than mindless enforcement of laws."

There's a daybook full of trenchant perceptions like those, worthy of highlighting, rereading regularly, and contemplating as you daily weave the tapestry of your own life. They confirm a belief that has set in concrete with me from exposure to thousands of officers across more than thirty years of writing about what it takes to survive and thrive on the street: Good cops are among the keenest students of human psychology I know.

The contributors to *If I Knew Then* have bequeathed us legacies of excellence, to steal a phrase that Brian Willis often uses in his training and writing. There's no one better to teach us than someone who's "been there." Their messages from the blazing pyre of experience can constitute a compass for young officers just starting their career trek, certainly. But they can also motivate any of us—LEO and civilian alike, age or years of service irrelevant—who still have breaths to draw and the courage to seek improvement.

If I could add a personal lesson learned, it would be this: Time rushes by. Too many of us will not truly *feel* that in our gut until our race is nearly run and we reflect on treasures squandered when time seemed endless.

"The tragedy of life," the philosopher W. M. Lewis has said, "is not that it ends too soon but that we wait too long to begin it." Whatever resonates with you as you read on, whatever prompts you to assess and refocus, remember: the clock is ticking.

—Charles Remsberg

Introduction

When I asked Chuck Remsberg if he would be willing to write the foreword for *If I Knew Then 2: Warrior Reflections*, he asked me what my reason or motivation was for putting together this book. Great question.

I have been blessed over the past 31 years since I started my law enforcement career. In that time, I have experienced the support of a loving family. I have worked with some great partners. I have worked for some strong leaders who have pushed me to grow as a person and law enforcement professional. I have supervised a number of amazing people who supported me, challenged me, encouraged me, and made me a better leader and a better trainer. I have received training from some of the best trainers in the world, who provided more than skills and tactics; they shared their insights and understanding, cultivated over years of training and real world experience, so I could better share what I had learned with others. I have received the support, friendship, mentoring, advice, and direction of so many great law enforcement and military officers, trainers, and leaders from across Canada, the U.S., and the U.K. I have had the privilege and honor of providing training to thousands of law enforcement professionals, many of whom have shared their stories and experiences with me. And now, I sit and ask myself, "How do I share that? How do I repay those that have given me so much? How do I help fellow law enforcement professionals learn the lessons of those warriors who have gone before them?"

The answer is through my speaking, my training, my writing, and through the books published through Warrior Spirit

Books—*If I Knew Then: Life Lessons from Cops on the Street* and *If I Knew Then 2: Warrior Reflections,* along with *W.I.N. Critical Issues in Training and Leading Warriors* and *W.I.N. 2 Insights into Training and Leading Warriors.*

I would like to share with you something written by a friend and fellow trainer who requested to remain anonymous. It is called, "Escape From Evanescence." Although it was written for law enforcement trainers, I would encourage you to read it a number of times and find a way to apply the message to your life.

Take care.

Brian Willis

Escape From Evanescence (The Trainer's Creed)

I looked throughout my life for a cause that could not and would not be evanescent. Evanescence means that when my life is gone, so too are my works. Disappearing like water drops on a scalding hot griddle.

I, like you, found my life's cause in my God, my family, work, and my training, to provide, to serve, to protect, and to strive continually.

We drive along life's path to its end. One of us will give our life for the cause every fifty hours. Yet, still we will…we…will…drive…on!

Our courage and our spirit do not hesitate in the hunt for both security of our various nations, and for quiet greatness. We accept what comes.

We find joy and comfort in living, working, and training, especially in our camaraderie of training. Take the time to lift the spirits of a sister or brother today and every day. There is definitely nothing evanescent there.

We are part of a larger and better organization. A group of brothers and sisters rivaled in legend and bigger than life who make us strive to be good enough to be on their shoulder "at the sharp end." People with whom we would willingly make a "live entry" through any door in the world.

Trainers and friends that are grand enough to drive us, help us when we fail, lend support and not judgment when we make the hard calls. To lift us when we fall and drive us when we falter.

In our positive attitude and training, we leave our legacy. Those we train will keep to the path and high expectations. And we hope those who follow will remember us well and find no fault. For in the end, we can only, and will only, do our best.

Literally, hundreds of thousands of officers and our many societies benefit from our experience, work, and training. The lives we save both individually and collectively are often unknown and forever remain unsung.

But in this grand association, this cohort of magnificent and capable legends, we revel. Let there never be mediocrity or a standard of "just good enough." The calling is too important and the stakes too abominably high.

There is no evanescence or ego here in this room among equals. Among women and men who are strong, capable, and driven.

May there never be. We call upon each other. Our hearts cry out to each other.

Be…the…legend.

Am I That Man?

By Ron Scheidt

After almost 20 years as a United States probation officer, I can still hear that ringing phone that started it all. On the other end of the line was Burt Matthies, then Chief U.S. Probation Officer of the District of Nebraska, who asked if I would accept a position with his office. It was a proud moment, a decision that would change my life forever and one I would never regret.

As I enter the 20th and final year as a Senior U.S. Probation Officer—a career that has been filled with tremendous satisfaction, numerous opportunities, and many wonderful memories—I find myself in a time of reflection. The thing I will miss the most is the relationships. Although I've established many wonderful friendships in my career, the two most defining relationships occurred early in my life and set the tone for allowing me to pursue this profession.

I wish I knew then that the most influential people in my life—my mentors and role models—had begun preparing me long before that phone call in 1991. They were the ones who put me in a position to begin my career with the United States government and never let me forget where I came from. They inspired me to become a man and a better person, even when I didn't feel like it, so as not to disappoint them. Their approval and acceptance meant the world to me.

My brother, Roger "Bud" Scheidt, was my role model and mentor long before I even knew what those words meant.

I grew up in a very dysfunctional family. My dad was a hard worker and an even harder drinker. Weekends were something to dread. My earliest memories of Bud were of him and his wife, Carolyn, picking me up as a young child and taking me to ballgames, movies, out to eat—anything to get me out of that environment. He was not only a brother; he was a father figure and best friend. His selflessness was my salvation. As an athlete, a marine, and a man, he was larger than life.

In my early adulthood, I had the opportunity to work in a steel plant alongside my brother, who was the production superintendent at the facility. I remember him commenting on many days how hungry he was and how much he was looking forward to the home-cooked lunch Carolyn had packed for him. It seemed that, more often than not, he ended up giving his food away to an employee who didn't have the means to bring his own food that day. And he always did it in such a way that left the employee thinking they had done Bud a favor. This is just one example of how he made the lives of everyone that he met better.

In June 1985, my brother was diagnosed with pancreatic cancer and given less than a year to live. I'll never forget a car ride that he and I took the night he realized that the treatments weren't working. The doctors had said there was nothing more they could do, and he needed to prepare for the end. Through the tears, I looked at him and asked, as I had so many times before, "What are we going to do?" And, for the first time in my life, the man who always had the answers said, "There's nothing we can do. But I'm not going to let something this small get me down." At his funeral six months later, as I stood to follow the recessional, I felt the eyes of all 800 attendees on me. I questioned then if I was that man.

Another important quality of a mentor is the ability to see potential in someone that they themselves can't. Bill Hunsaker, my junior high school physical education teacher and basketball coach, saw that in me. Following my father's death at age 13, Coach seemed to understand innately my need for direction as a young male innately. At a pivotal point in my life, he invested time and interest in me. I wanted to be just like him, so when he recommended I attend college to follow my dream of teaching and coaching, I did it without hesitation. Without his encouragement, my current position in the field of criminal justice would have been unattainable. More than 40 years later, Coach and I still talk several times a week, and I always seem to walk away with another life lesson. If you know Mayberry sheriff Andy Griffith, the television character, then you know Coach, too. He continues to be a role model and an inspiration to me. I consider Coach to be among the biggest influences in my life, and I often wonder, "Am I that man?"

Of course, there are many other men and women both inside and outside the criminal justice profession who have touched my life, and whose words and actions still resonate with me today. But I will tell you that in your real relationships the people who leave their imprint in your life years later will do so in their own way. I may not remember everything that these individuals said or did, but I will never forget how they made me feel.

Think about those people in your life, and thank them for helping you get where you are today in your career and as a person. Then consider if you are that person for someone else. If you were fortunate enough to be blessed with a Bud or Coach already in your life as I was, cherish and nurture that relationship. If not, I would encourage you to seek individuals actively and intentionally that will enhance your life and challenge your growth professionally, personally, and spiritually. I often wonder where I would be today if Bud and Coach hadn't invested in me and modeled in their own unique ways what it meant to be a man, a father, an employee, and a friend. Find that special person in your life. Those relationships—more than any career accomplishments—are what you will never forget.

I encourage you to look outward; and never stop asking yourself, "Are you that man?"

Ron Scheidt is a Senior United States Probation Officer with the District of Nebraska. He currently serves as the agency's Training Specialist, Program Development Coordinator, Defensive Tactics Instructor, and Tactical Response Team Leader. In addition, Ron supervises a case load of high-risk federal offenders.

Ron serves as a guest presenter and instructor on defensive tactics, officer safety and street survival tactics at conferences and academies nationwide, and has trained community corrections officers from all 50 states. Upon retirement, Ron will assume the position as Lead Defensive Tactics Instructor with the Community Corrections Institute, a business whose mission is to provide relevant and realistic training to community corrections professionals. He can be reached at ron@scheidtgroup.com.

Crafting a Positive Culture of Training

By Timothy Patton

"What is one key piece of advice you would give to a new officer starting out today?" This is the question posed by Brian Willis as a means of soliciting advice for new recruits and officers in their FTO phase. To this question I would reply, "Take the lead in your own training and development. Demand the same of your colleagues and your department. Identify obstacles to learning, and take action towards their elimination. Play an active role in your department's culture of training and continue to ask, 'What's next?'"

September Training

It's the middle of September 2010 and a group of officers and sergeants has gathered at the department's new training facility for a series of scenarios. The first simulated call has two officers responding to assist a third who has been shot in the leg and is currently pinned down behind a piece of cover. The suspect has run into a shed within view of the downed officer. As the responding officers arrive on scene and begin to assess the situation, the suspect fires a shot towards the downed officer who is now reporting that he has lost significant blood and fears he will pass out. The suspect is armed with a training handgun, firing marking projectiles. The responding officers are armed with the same and have access to AR15s, which also fire marking projectiles. Numerous officers have completed the scenario utilizing a variety of techniques to make a hasty and dangerous rescue of the downed officer—the objective of the scenario. Some chose to move as a team, keeping one officer out front with the AR15 while the second served as a dragger. Others set up a fixed firing position with the AR15 while their partner dashed out to make the rescue. Most fired at the suspect as he peeked from the shed door to shoot and some chose to utilize directed fire to the doorway to protect them during the rescue. The final pair however, remained behind their own cover and engaged in a protracted gun battle with the suspect in the shed while the downed officer cried for help until directed to go silent, simulating a loss of consciousness. Ultimately, the scenario was ended and the officers were asked to discuss their plan and evaluate the tactics they employed. Once complete, a sergeant asked if they had considered any type of rescue of the downed officer. The more senior officer quickly replied, "That would have directly contradicted the training I received in the academy." He went on to cite his initial active shooter training and the necessity to have a minimum of four officers present prior to moving forward to engage an active threat. The officer did not appear to give any serious consideration to the tactics proposed by the instructors. The instructors did not seem prepared to deal with this possible outcome, and instead let the officers walk away with a performance that all agreed was less than optimal. It should be noted that the academy training referred to by the officer took place in 1996, while the in-service active shooter training occurred in late 2000. Specific training on officer-down rescues had taken place since 2000, but never in teams as small as two officers.

All of the participants in this training were well intentioned. The sergeant instructors identified a series of objectives as an optimal response to a dangerous situation that entailed a certain degree of risk. The officers who participated did so out of their own desire to learn or, in some cases, simply because they were asked to do so by a superior. My fellow training team members and I participated out of a desire to support more on-duty training initiatives. Unfortunately, we collectively fell short of our objectives. Rather than arming these officers with better tactics, we allowed them to walk away from training with lingering doubts not only in their skills, but also in our ability to teach.

Lessons Learned

This scenario and debrief, while unique, exemplify the challenges of continued learning, and emphasize the role of the culture of training.

First, let's examine the defensiveness of the officer in question. Even recruits in the academy, who are thought of as eager learners, demonstrate unease with critical feedback. A small number of our officers indicate difficulty sleeping the night before in-service due to anxiety. While these feelings towards training are understandable, the negative outcome of avoiding training and learning, or ineffective teaching is unacceptable in a profession where failure to learn can be deadly. Negative feelings associated with training can be caused by many things, but include individual lack of confidence, poorly planned or implemented training and teaching styles that are overbearing and evaluative rather than instructional. Regardless of the source of opposition, all members of the department must work to eliminate these issues in order to ensure that our valuable training hours are as constructive as possible.

Next, think back to the officer citing training that occurred over a decade earlier as the basis for his chosen tactic. While this may demonstrate a simple desire to shift the blame, we must also examine the speed with which the tactics of law enforcement and suspects alike have changed. The Columbine tragedy of 1999 forever changed law enforcement tactics and spawned the development of four-person contact teams. Just 10 short years later, references to paired and even solo-officer responses are cited in law enforcement periodicals across the country. This officer, in this scenario seemed to be saying, "I didn't do it, because you didn't train me to." My question to the officer is this: To whom should we charge the responsibility of keeping up with the forever-changing landscape of tactics and training? A training division cannot be relied upon as the sole source of information. Individual officers must take the lead in their own training and development. Twenty-four hours of mandatory in-service can not possibly keep one up-to-speed on all that is changing in our field. To this end, the department must actively support information gathering and sharing. It is not enough to send a select few to trainings of their choosing. The department must strategically guide this information gathering by topic and must facilitate the sharing of these lessons in a timely fashion. Personal responsibility is necessary but not sufficient. Department structure and processes are necessary but not sufficient. A truly successful training program requires both.

Finally, when we observe a less than optimal performance—be it during a scenario, on the range during in-service, or on the street—we must identify the subcomponents of the performance and formulate a plan to address the issues highlighted. Anything less is simply an example of negligence. As those officers walked away from that training in September, all of the parties involved allowed a faulty culture of training to be the excuse for the performance itself and the lack of follow-through. Excuses are easy.

- How can they expect me to do that when they never trained me?
- That officer is like that—he doesn't like to train. There's no need to do another rep.
- The sergeant instructors are new—they shouldn't be expected to have a plan to deal with an extraordinary response.
- We don't have time to develop training to deal with this negative outcome.

Again, excuses are easy. Too often, the challenges of training and learning are pointed to as the reasons why we should not try new things or should not expect more out of each other and ourselves. The training in September is far too often accepted as the norm. We can break this cycle and create a new culture. There is greatness among us and within us all. Our training and development are far too important to be left to chance and the shifting makeup of any training division. Individual officers, those assigned to training, and the department as a whole, can make a positive difference in this area that ensures our success. Regardless of one's position and role in the department's training program, personal responsibility is essential. It is our approach to learning that will accurately predict our future. We must individually and collectively recognize what we don't know. We must seek and accept feedback, and remain committed to growth over time. It is our collective culture of training that determines how we will respond and what our capacity is to meet the challenges of our ever-changing field.

How to Positively Influence the Culture of Training

Officers, instructors, trainers, and departments can all positively influence the culture of training.

To individual officers:
- Stay up-to-speed on national trends, including both suspect and officer tactics. One good source is the website, www.officer.com.
- Develop a training log that captures annual training hours, topics, lessons learned, unanswered questions, certifications, etc.
- Create a Training Wish List of outside trainings that you would like to attend. Submit requests to attend these trainings and develop a plan for how you could share the information with other members of your department.
- Take part in your department's culture of training. Volunteer as an actor for reality-based trainings. Develop a tabletop training to be shared with members of your platoon.
- Share a sample of your reports on a quarterly basis with a trusted colleague, detective, or detective lieutenant for review and suggestions.
- Debrief your calls with other officers and constantly search for tactics that result in optimal outcomes with minimal exposure to risk.

To instructors and trainers:
- Employ and teach a Student-Centered Debriefing model for use with scenario-based instruction. This method of debriefing results in better learning as well as a more optimistic outlook on instruction and feedback. A good example is available from FLETC.

- Teach recruits and officers what they *can* do. Teach in the positive and find alternatives to the word, "Don't."
- Compare tactics based on outcomes and risks, as opposed to "right and wrong."
- Develop a plan for dealing with personnel who experience high levels of anxiety during training. One possible strategy is Performance Enhancement Imagery.
- Plan for a wide range of responses to scenarios and build in time for re-dos where necessary. It is essential for participants to end on a good repetition.
- Take chances; try different things and risk failure. Nothing gives perspective like screwing up something and nothing enables officers to succeed more than an atmosphere that is tolerant and even expectant of failure.

To departments:
- Task a variety of personnel throughout the department with identifying the future of the department's training needs. Constantly ask, "What's next?"
- Encourage personnel to seek out and attend outside trainings. As a part of this process, set clear expectations for the participant to bring the knowledge gained back to the department.
- Identify the most common obstacles to learning and develop strategies to combat them. Involve all levels of the department in this task.
- Make training a shared responsibility.

Timothy J. Patton is an officer with the City of Madison Police Department, Madison Wisconsin. He was hired in 2002 and is currently assigned to the Personnel and Training Team as a Training Officer, Lead Instructor in Patrol Rifle, and Vehicle Contacts and Recruit Scenario-Based Instructor. His certifications include Force Science Certification, DAAT, Firearms, and Sub-Gun Instructor. He has been a member of the Department's SWAT Entry Platoon since 2005. Tim was formerly a high school special education teacher and soccer coach. He is married with two children.

The Critics

By Jim Nieman

They seem to resent even the knowledge of our existence. Perhaps denial of the violence and danger in our world makes them feel secure. Perhaps the fact that they depend on us for protection irritates them and makes them feel inferior. Indeed they look upon us with scorn and belittle the work we do—work they do not have the constitution to do themselves. Yet because they cannot alone defend themselves and their loved ones, they are the very soft underbellies that the predators seek. The critics would rather we hide in the shadows so as not to interfere with the harmony of their existence until they need us. But then, when the time comes, when the evil they deny enters their peaceful existence, we had best be there to do that which they cannot, and our appearance must be immediate. For now, we are their best friends and the most essential element of their society as they cower in the safety of our shadow while we do what we have trained and committed to do.

But then, as the darkness gives way to the light of day and reveals the violence of the necessary resolution, the heartfelt appreciation begins to fade. Their urgent need for protection has been replaced with an air of superiority, and they look at us and what we do with distaste. They see it as uncivilized and unnecessary; they can't understand why we would choose this path. They have never stood in the sand of the arena and felt the sting of tears and sweat, or the taste of blood. They will never feel the fear of battle or the loss of a fellow warrior. They cannot appreciate sense of duty or the satisfaction of doing something that may be difficult, dangerous, and uncertain but necessary. They have never felt true brotherhood and the shared pain of those who have stood shoulder to shoulder. They can never appreciate the sacrifice made by those who have given all in the fight on behalf of those who neither understand nor appreciate.

However, it is not enough for them to simply lack understanding. Instead, in the safe light of the day, they now turn to criticism and scorn of the very thing they needed done but were unable to do themselves. Their criticisms will not offer the warriors realistic alternatives or solutions, only unrealistic expectations and constraints that could only come from ignorance. Their society cannot function without us and yet they strive to tie the very hands that protect them. They will congratulate themselves on their civilized solutions and demand adherence from the warriors who know only too well how ineffective their solutions will be. The warrior's objections will fall on deaf ears. How do you make someone understand the blinding speed of escalating violence, the rush of adrenaline, and the cascade of stimulus upon which you must base split-second decisions? How do you explain the fear you feel to your very core as you step forward knowing that is the only direction you can go because you have sworn to do so and that oath means something to you that they could never understand. Furthermore, they will never appreciate why you would even want to do what you do. They will never feel the strength of the bond of brotherhood, or understand the commitment to this calling.

So what do we do with this information? Why do we continue to do what we do? First, we must remember that this sentiment comes only from those critics who live in a dark and bitter world. They see everything through the inside of their smudged "half empty" glass and we should pity them for that. They will not know what they have missed until it is too late, and maybe not even then. We do not do this job for them. We do it because we recognize the opportunity to step forward and challenge ourselves to do the right thing. This is a worthy calling and we are not too timid to overcome our fears and step up because we know what must be done. But, we also understand what it means to commit ourselves to a cause and we know the satisfaction that comes with that. We also know that even in defeat, after having given our best, there is victory and satisfaction in knowing you have done all you can. There is no victory for those who never try, for those who instead attempt to satisfy the empty soul with criticism for those who have had the courage they lack.

We also do it because we know that these critics may be the loudest, but they are not the majority. We know that the majority, even if they are silent and cannot appreciate or understand all that we do, value us. They do not like the fact that our society relies on us and what we must do, but they understand the necessity. They may not have the desire or the ability to do what we do, but they still understand that they sleep safely at night because of us. Just ask them to imagine a day without critics and politicians making policies and laws and then compare that to a day without warriors standing guard and enforcing those laws as they keep the predators at bay. Ask them to take a moment to think about those days and what it would really be like. Which would they choose?

On a personal level, I wish I had not given the critics the energy I have over the course of my career. They will never be satisfied and that should never be our goal. Instead, I wish I had learned to have more appreciation for some of the brothers and sisters that I have worked with over the years earlier on, many of whom are still out there doing this job for reasons that even we must question at times. And what of the mentors, leaders, and trainers who have gone before us, and those who still guide and inspire us today? One of the most understated privileges of our work is the opportunity to access some of the most dedicated and knowledgeable people in the world. It took me a long time to discover them, and they will never profess their greatness to anyone. They just do what they do because they believe in it and know that it is the right thing to do. Some have never worn a uniform but their commitment to those who do is unquestionable. The most satisfying years of my career have been during my time as a trainer and being able to learn from some of these individuals. These are truly great people and, although I do not profess to count myself among them, I do hope I have influenced some of the people I have trained in some small way and shared some of the valuable lessons I have learned. Just knowing I have passed on even a fraction of what I have learned from these people is enough. I wish I had paid more attention to them years ago when I thought I knew so much.

This is often a thankless and frustrating occupation and doing it right seems to get more impossible every day; but we need to turn our focus away from the criticism and appreciate the things that make it special. And that is the opportunity to do something worthwhile and, at the same time, work and learn with some of the most dedicated and honorable people you will ever meet. Having an appreciation for some of these individuals and what this career really means makes the voice of the critic sound empty and meaningless. I wish I would have known then what I know now.

Jim Nieman has spent 33 years as a member of the Royal Canadian Mounted Police. He has worked in a variety of locations from the largest detachments in the lower mainland of British Columbia to some of the smallest in Canada's arctic. Training in the tactical and firearms area became his passion about halfway through his career and remains so today. All of his service has been operational except for his most recent last couple years, which he has spent working in the national headquarters in Ottawa in the Use of Force Program.

Jim has devoted his final years of his career to reminding as many people as he can, as often as is necessary, that we must never lose sight of our real purpose and obligation: to support the men and women who step forward every day to do this difficult job.

Developing Expertise While Maintaining the Work-life Balance

By Chris Lawrence

While a police officer's career can provide a wide variety of stimulation and opportunity to be involved in meaningful work, home fires and other aspects of a normal life compete for the officer's time and attention. The battle between live-to-work or work-to-live remains ever present.

Policing is a career that carries very real risks, different from those experienced in civilian life. During my operational career, one colleague was stabbed to death while taking a bogus break-and-enter report. Another was disarmed and shot by an individual he was checking out in an alley. A third was slashed across the throat by a person he thought was a victim of a robbery. Other occupations don't often involve *clients* who kill. In the year 2010, 60 police officers in the U.S. and one in Canada were killed by subjects. At the same time, 73 U.S. and 3 Canadian officers died in traffic related accidents. (From The Washington Post and Officer Down Memorial Page, Inc.) Whether involved in roadside traffic stops, directing traffic on busy multi-lane streets, or trying to stop a fleeing felon, traffic related accidents represent an under appreciated threat to the men and women of law enforcement.

Stress is yet another insidious threat to the health of police personnel. During a recent dinner with a group of very experienced police officers, a police manager responsible for the Human Resource portfolio within his agency (which counts their officers by the tens of thousands), posed a question: "How many monthly pension cheques does one of our 35-year veterans collect prior to their death?" I was shocked to learn the answer was, on average, only nine. That's less than a year! If an officer retired by their early 50s, life expectancy increased to an additional 25 years. The stress of policing can kill you. That is, if you allow it.

Each officer owes it to their family to develop expertise in many areas such as police procedures, communications skills, threat assessment, and driving. Your best weapon is your mouth well engaged with your brain and for the majority of officers their most frequent activity is operating a patrol car. Although newer officers may never have heard of him, Buck Savage taught us long ago to "Watch the Hands!" Driving instructors have told us to "look ahead: plan ahead," and to ensure we save space for an escape route. In addition to these skill sets, the individual officer needs to balance work with life so that he or she can live to collect their well-earned retirement.

In the past, the problem with developing expertise was that you had to work at it. It takes 10,000 hours of deliberate practice to develop expertise in any domain (Ericsson et. al 2006). That means more than just going through the motions. While repetition and practice is the one constant that will improve a skill set, it does not necessarily develop expertise. The difference comes from understanding the events that lead up to performance, how they can be broken down, and what lessons can be learned (Starkes and Ericsson 2003). Given all the competing processes and considerations, how can a police officer develop his or her expertise and still maintain a balance in their life?

The good news is that expertise can be developed and you can enhance the requisite development during your regular duties simply by paying attention to your *practice*. Like physicians, police officers cannot perform every technical detail perfectly in every situation. The human race is too varied; the circumstances police deal with daily are full of too many unknowns. You must practice the art of policing as well as study the science associated with it. You can practice your profession every hour you are at work.

As for studying the art, every call you go to, every interaction you have, provides an opportunity to learn. Policing is no different from any other undertaking—there is a learning process. No academy provides a recruit with everything he or she will need to be successful in their career. You need to pay attention to your peers and trainers. You also need to think and listen to yourself. In doing so, you can begin your journey towards expertise. Even well into your career, you can look back on your experiences and try to make sense of what you have seen and heard. It's never too late to start.

One of the best examples of a learning opportunity, based on my experience, is the time you spend driving and the traffic accidents you investigate. You get to look into mistakes made by others on a routine basis. Once you have made the situation safe and have collected the details of the event, reflect back on what was said by the drivers and witnesses. After a while, you will see patterns develop. While you are driving, look ahead for potential problems that might develop at intersections, on and off ramps, and parking lot entrances and exits. While doing traffic enforcement, watch how drivers interact with their environment. I believe it has made me a better driver. I'm confident it has allowed me to avoid situations that otherwise would have resulted in a collision.

If you are interested in learning more about traffic accidents, related investigations, or driving motor vehicles, the internet can provide lots of direction on where you can find further information (for example, a four page bibliography of related texts is available at http://www.jibc.ca/library/Bibliographies/Traffic_Accident_Investigation_-_JIBC_Library.pdf [accessed January 10, 2011]). If traffic investigations do not interest you, other areas can be explored: frauds, crime scene investigation, use of force—the limitations are your own imagination and the size and sophistication of your agency. Even small police services provide for the development of expertise in a variety of topics.

The point is, much of the time required to develop expertise in any area is going to occur anyway and you have a front row seat in "The Open Police University" (Lawrence 2010, 195-202) Making the most of it will provide your career with meaning of your choosing. As you progress through your personal education, keep in mind that one of the best ways to learn, after you master the skills, is to teach others. I find I learn more by having to teach a topic than learning it in a more traditional, passive manner. Writing can accomplish much of the same goal. The process of writing down the precise steps to take and the rationale as to why those steps are in the order they are, can be quite challenging. It can also cause you to reconsider your past assumptions and beliefs.

I developed an early interest in officer safety and related procedures. I had the good fortune to start my police career in a small city less than 10 miles from one of North America's premier police training facilities, the Ontario Police College. The instructors were very helpful and the facility was a warehouse of knowledge and opportunities for learning.

Sage advice was given early: "Pay attention, there's a lot to learn. The knowledge you gain came at an awful price."

Over the years, a personal procedure has developed. Each anniversary of my career start date, June 5th, I reflect on the year just past: what have I learned? What do I need to work on? Where do I go from here? Every five years I stop and take stock. Have I accomplished my goals? Am I on a solid path? I also reflect on the whole of my progress since the last five-year check-up. What I discovered about myself in the context of officer safety may help you. After five years, I felt pretty confident in my skill set. I was well trained, very interested in my career, and very active in my practice. At the 10-year mark, I looked back on what I knew after 5 years and how much more I knew after 10. I felt really confident. At the 15-year mark, I understood how little I really knew about the art of policing. Or, should I say, there were many more questions than answers.

The sobering effect for me was that, according to research conducted by the FBI, based on events from 1981 through 1990, 31% of officers killed had one to five years of experience while 39% had six to 10 years. The remaining officers had 10 or more years of experience. With respect to my three colleagues who died, the first officer had five years experience; the second had eight, while the third officer had an 18-year career.

I continue to practice my skill-set and spend time learning about the science of policing with a focus on police use of force and related procedures. My career requires that I do it. That can provide the necessary time for my family and the distractions I enjoy. Along the way, I teach, write, and discuss my practice with others within a community of practice (Bloom 2004, 20-22). I still reflect back on my career of over 30 years to ensure that I'm moving forward. I hope I beat the odds and enjoy more than 9 months of retirement. I'd prefer to see reaching pensionable age as a milestone rather than a precursor to a tombstone.

By exploiting the time you will spend engaged in your career, and paying attention to what is going on around you, you enhance your ability to develop expertise in the area of policing that you choose. The art of policing should be practiced. The additional time required to develop your knowledge of the science of policing can be managed such that its impact on the rest of your life is reduced. Time is still available to attend to things that really matter: your family, your health (including fighting the effects of stress), as well as the time to enjoy our brief period upon this earth. You can start right now, experience notwithstanding.

Works Cited

> C. Lawrence, "The Open Police University," in *If I Knew Then: Life Lessons From Cops on the Street,* ed. Brian R. Willis. (Calgary, AB: Warrior Spirit Books, 2010).
> G. Bloom, and R. Stein. "Leadership" in *Building Communities of Practice, (2004)* 20-22.
> Flaherty, Mary Pat. 2010. "Officer line of duty deaths up in 2010." *The Washington Post*, December 28. Accessed January 10, 2011. http://voices.washingtonpost.com/crime-scene/around-the-nation/officer-line-of-duty-deaths-up.html.
> J. L. Starkes and K. A. Ericsson. *Expert Performance in Sports: Advances in Research on Sport Expertise* (Champaign, IL: Human Kinetics, 2003).
> K. A. Ericsson, N. Charness, P. J. Feltovich, and R.R. Hoffman. *The Cambridge Handbook of Expertise*

and *Expert Performance* (New York: Cambridge University Press, 2006).

The Officer Down Memorial Page, Inc. 2010. "Honoring Officers Killed in the Year 2010." Accessed January 10, 2011. http://www.odmp.org/canada/year.php?year=2010

With over 30 years of police-related experience, Chris's past assignments include Patrol, Underwater Search and Recovery, Marine Enforcement, Tactical and Rescue Unit, Criminal Investigation, and Training in one of Canada's largest municipal police services.

Since 1996, Chris has been an instructor at the Ontario Police College, one of North America's largest police training facilities. Chris was also seconded to the Canadian Police Research Centre where he was assigned as a Project Manager for research involving Less-Lethal Weapons, In-Custody Death, and Personal Protective Equipment.

Chris holds a Master's degree in Leadership and Training, specializing in Justice and Public Safety from British Columbia's Royal Roads University. Since 2004, he has been a Technical Advisor to Force Science Institute Ltd. at Minnesota State University, Mankato, and is a member of the Canadian Law Enforcement Forum.

He has presented on police use of force and sudden in-custody deaths throughout North America, Australia, and Europe, to police executives, investigators, trainers, and line officers, and medical and legal staff. Chris has also provided expert evidence in several North American jurisdictions and authored many articles related to these subjects.

Don't Treat Your Kids Like Suspects

By Leonard Dafoe

On June 1, 2010, after almost thirty years of challenging and often emotionally perplexing assignments, I retired from the Calgary Police Service, the only adult job I have ever known. Naturally, while attending university in Ottawa, I had part time and summer jobs in order to pay tuition, rent, and occasionally beer. Okay, tuition and rent often took a back seat to beer, but you get the idea. In 1979, my beautiful girlfriend, now my beautiful wife, and I left Ottawa for the wide-open spaces and ski hills of Western Canada. Our genius plan was to ski for a year or two and then return to university and become more or less permanent students. For unknown reasons, perhaps it was the rent, car payments, ski passes and, once again, beer, we found that life in Calgary was really, really expensive and thus we were both forced to seek gainful employment. At that time, the Calgary Police Service appeared to be having serious difficulty attracting quality candidates and in 1980, with standards apparently dropping through the floor and into the basement, I was hired as a probationary constable. The rest, as they say, is history. During the subsequent three decades, I served as a uniformed constable and then as a member of our Strike Force Unit. Surprisingly, I was promoted to the rank of Detective and went on to work in the Organized Crime Section, Vice Unit, General Investigations, and then, just to demonstrate that irony is never far from our lives as police officers, my last two years were spent as an investigator in the Internal Affairs Unit.

I offer this chronicle of my ancient past only as a means to introduce my topic for Brian Willis's latest publication and promise that I will now get to the point. When I retired, I wrote a letter to the 10-4 magazine, a publication put out by the Calgary Police Association, and included, with apologies to David Letterman, a top ten list of life rules that I thought might offer some important insights for success as a police officer and human being. Brian contacted me soon afterwards and asked if I would try to condense my list to fit the general topic; "One thing you know now that you wish you had known at the start of your career." If only everything in life was so easy. In about three seconds, I realized that I wished I had known in 1980 that Microsoft stock, which probably sold for about five cents a share then, would one day be worth a million times more! I would have sold my kidneys and used the cash to buy all the shares I could in the then unknown computer company. Of course, by now I would be a gazillionaire and would have more than enough money for dialysis treatments.

Unfortunately, that brilliant bit of hindsight didn't make the original list; but I will endeavor to give the original list and then try to decide which of these gems is the "One Thing."

The List

1. I don't care if you have 10 years or 10 minutes on the job. Get professional financial planning advice (hint: Lotto 6-49 and Lotto Max do NOT qualify as financial planning strategies).

2. We are blessed to have this job, but be prepared to walk away from it if it becomes too damaging to your health and/or personal relationships; the organization will survive quite nicely without you, no one is irreplaceable. They will not name a day of the week after you if you keel over and die at your desk.

3. Do not be a cop at home, nor a parent at work.
4. Never argue with idiots, it is wasted time and energy you will never get back… Especially if the idiot is your boss.
5. Develop and maintain as many outside interests and friendships as possible.
6. Don't let your ego get you killed.
7. Treat each other with respect even though some of us try very, very hard to demonstrate that we aren't worthy of it.
8. Play nice in the sand box.
9. For god's sake, don't gossip!
10. Try to remember that life is short and should be enjoyed at every opportunity. Laugh, give a hug to a person who needs it, and don't take yourself so damned serious—Psychological Services is busy enough.

As I wrote this back in March, I noticed that more often than not I had failed to adhere to my own advice on rule number 3. As the father of a beautiful young girl, I was absolutely paranoid that she would be abducted by pimps, intergalactic slave traders, or assaulted and impregnated by bike gang members. It did not help that at the time she was becoming physically mature I was working as a child prostitution investigator in the Vice Unit. By then I had witnessed first hand the various ways and means that a young boy or girl could be reduced to a piece of meat and sold by the pound. To say that my experiences led to me making life difficult for my daughter is an understatement. I can't tell you the number of young men whose names I ran on CPIC (totally against department policy of course but show me a cop who hasn't), or the times I said the following to one of the poor unfortunates she managed to get through my initial screening process: "I have a shovel, a shotgun and an acreage. Behave yourself or get a one way tour of the acreage from inside a burlap sack."

The irony of this though is that all the while I was acting this way at home, at work I was desperately trying to save children from their past. Children involved in the sex trade were not there because they had failed algebra and could no longer qualify for NASA. And they certainly weren't in the sex trade because they had an insatiable desire to be the focus of violent sex acts at the hands of smelly, unstable, and often diseased strangers. My work had led me to understand that the majority of persons involved in the sex trade, children and adults, had been sexually, physically, or emotionally abused by a relative or some other trusted adult.

My life during this period became a dichotomy. I became a miserable, hard-assed cop-like father at home but, at work, I was an understanding, approachable substitute father for kids rescued from the sex trade. I was convinced that if I was able to show these children that not every adult male was a sexual predator it would contribute to their eventual healing. In doing so I failed to notice that the needs of these children—24-hour pager contacts, endless emergency phone calls and visits to safe houses, program meetings, court appearances, hospital visits, interviews and other dramatic interventions—were fast becoming the defining characteristics of my life. The more I clamped down at home and the more my daughter and I argued, the less she wanted to do with me. My validation came from the fact that all these damaged kids needed me and I proceeded to put all my energies where I thought they were needed. My arrogance and tunnel vision continued unabated for several years. My daughter grew up and moved out; the kids I worked with didn't seem to get any better. Some died, some disappeared, and some left the sex trade because they were just too sick to keep going. Few if any really responded in the long run to my "parental substitute" approach. My eventual acceptance of this dysfunctional situation came, not in a blinding flash of light or in a dramatic epiphany of sudden understanding, but rather as a gradual, self-induced metaphorical slap to the head. The idea that would eventually become rule number 3 evolved from this slow process of understanding.

I believe that, other than your spouse, the most important and significant relationship you will ever have is with your kids, and there is an inherent duty in that relationship to provide them with all the love and support possible. Anything that interferes in this relationship is bad by definition and you should avoid it at all costs. Being a cop requires us to adapt to negative stimuli in our environment and we often become emotionally hardened, rigid, overly critical, and (understandably) overly sensitive to threats of physical security. Elements of this workplace maladaptation inevitably creep into our personal lives. I thought I was immune to it, but the process was so insidious that I failed to notice my descent into stupidity.

Fortunately, for me, it has not been too late to rescue my relationship with my daughter. She is a tough, resilient, and very smart young lady who went on to graduate from university and appears to have forgiven me of my overly protective reign of fatherly terror. She married one of the fellas who, in a Darwinian fashion, survived my screening process and subtle death threats.

There it is. The one thing I truly know now but wished I had known at the beginning of my career. It is the importance of separating your work and personal life as much as is possible. Don't treat your kids like suspects and don't treat suspects like your kids. Both are recipes for personal and professional disaster. Good luck in your careers, and stay safe.

Len began his career with the Calgary Police Service in 1980 and retired in 2010 after 30 years of service. During his career, he was fortunate to serve in many different capacities, but his favorite assignments were always those where he had the opportunity to be a mentor to junior members. This concern for peers and subordinates alike lead him to become involved in the Peer Support and Critical Incident Stress Management programs. His concern for the health and personal welfare of his peers has always transcended his other professional interests.

In 2008, Len completed a Masters degree in Ethno-Political Conflict Analysis. He has spent the last two years working in Africa for the Pearson Peacekeeping Centre. As a facilitator for the United Nations Police Pre-Deployment and Sexual and Gender Based Violence programs, he has had the opportunity to assist African Union peacekeepers in preparing for their mission in Darfur.

Despite his almost total lack of charm and personality, the same lovely lady he met in a university Exercise Physiology class in 1977 has remained with him. They have one incredible daughter and several strange dogs.

Everyone is a Leader

By Brian Willis

I was 22 years old when I started my law enforcement career and I had a great deal to learn about life, about being a law enforcement professional and about leadership. Like a lot of people, I thought leadership was about rank, title, and position in an organization. I thought that the leaders of the organization were the Sergeants, Inspectors, Lieutenants, Captains, Superintendents, and Chiefs. Over the years, I learned many valuable lessons about leadership. I learned that leadership is not about rank, position, or title. Leadership is about action and interaction. Leadership is about doing what's right, not what's popular. Leadership is about doing what's right, not what's expedient. Perhaps the most important lesson I have learned over the years is that *everyone* in an organization is in a position to lead.

Throughout my career, I observed, and at times participated in, the continual and excessive complaining and finger pointing. I have seen too many officers get caught up in the blame game where instead of looking for solutions, they are continually looking for someone to blame. As cops, we often spend a great deal of time and energy complaining.

We complain about…

- The "lack of leadership" at the top of the organization;
- The 'fact' we have too many managers and not enough leaders, yet few can actually explain what they mean by that;

- The fact that we do not get enough training, and then we complain when we get assigned to attend training;
- The equipment we have, the equipment we used to have, and the equipment we should have;
- The vehicles we are assigned, how the equipment is laid out in them, and how no one takes responsibility for keeping them clean;
- The facilities or lack thereof;
- The citizens who don't appreciate us;
- The justice system;
- The cops on the other shifts;
- Patrol officers complain about the specialty units and the specialty units complain about the patrol officers;
- And, of course, we complain about the shift schedule.

The point of this article is to encourage you to take the first step toward being a leader. Step away from the blame game, stop pointing fingers, and stop waiting for someone else to take action. It is important throughout your career to focus on what *you* control. Focus on what *you* can do to make a difference. Accept that, regardless of your position in your organization, you are in a position to lead, to train yourself and others, and to make a difference.

It is my experience over the last 30 years that many of the major changes in organizations started at the grass roots level. These significant changes are driven from the bottom up, not from the top down. The officers in the field know what works and what does not. They know what they need for equipment and training. They know what needs to be done at a particular call to make it safer for the people that are there. They know because they are there. They know because they are at the pointy end of the stick. They know because they do the job every day. The ones that understand leadership take action to initiate change.

I have learned over the years that leadership is about stepping up and speaking up. If you are at a call and you see that something is not going right then be a leader and speak up. You may have seen something others did not and your willingness to take action and speak up may save a life. If you are a supervisor or a senior officer on a shift, then encourage the younger officers to speak up at debriefings and at calls when they see something that is dangerous or something that can be improved. The junior person on the shift may not have years of experience (although, you may be surprised at the experience they do have), but in many cases the most junior people have the most up-to-date training. Now, let's be very clear. I am not advocating questioning every decision the Sergeant makes or continually challenging your senior partner because you think he or she is a dinosaur. Being a leader is about knowing when to step up, when to speak up, and when to shut up.

If you see something that could be improved in your agency, put together an action plan with potential solutions and put it forward to someone who has the authority to approve it or is willing to take it to higher levels for approval. If you see a gap in training, then do some research and put forward some possible solutions on how those gaps might be filled. Better yet, get involved as a trainer for your organization.

It is important to remember that no one buys anything (cars, houses, your proposals,) based on why it is important to you. Learn to step back and put yourself in the other person's position, and then sell it to them based on why it is important to them. I would also encourage you to read the book "Switch: How to Change Things When Change is Hard" by Chip and Dan Heath (2010).

Remember to be patient. Change does not happen overnight. Some of the changes I had the pleasure of being involved in orchestrating took years to bring to fruition. A few months ago, I spent some time on the phone with a leader and trainer I have a great amount of respect and admiration for. She works in an emergency services communications centre and is continually attending courses and seminars at her own expense to expand her knowledge and skills. She then takes what she has learned and shares it with her co-workers. She has been working tirelessly for more than a year to change the culture of negativity that was becoming pervasive in her workplace and after all this time she is making headway. She is a leader not because of her title, but because of her actions, and she is making an impact on the culture of the organization.

I wish I had known at the start of my career that *everyone* is in...
- A position to lead;
- A position to train others;
- A position to make a difference.

Two questions you need to ask yourself:
1. What's important now?
2. Are you are going to choose to lead?

Given the choice between spending your career as a problem identifier or a problem solver, choose to be a problem solver. Choose to be a leader.

Brian Willis is an internationally recognized thought leader, speaker, and trainer. He draws upon his 25 years of law enforcement experience as a member of the Calgary Police Service and 20 years of training experience to provide cutting-edge training to law enforcement officers and trainers throughout North America. Brian operates the innovative training company Winning Mind Training, and is the editor of the highly acclaimed books "W.I.N.: Critical Issues in Training and Leading Warriors" (2008), "W.I.N. 2 Insights Into Training and Leading Warriors"(2009), and "If I Knew Then: Life Lessons From Cops on the Street" (2010); www.warriorspiritbooks.com. Brian serves as the Deputy Executive Director for !LEETA and is a member of NTOA, ITOA, IALEFI, and the Canadian Association of Professional Speakers. Brian can be reached through his website at www.winningmindtraining.com.

For the Right Reasons

By Ed Nowicki

Do you want to become a police officer in order to become a hero? If so, become a firefighter. Everyone loves firefighters, since they save people's lives and stop fires from burning down their homes. Most of the time as a police officer, you serve as society's grim reaper. You are the one that has to tell families that a family member was arrested, was injured, or just died. Police officers are required to deal with the negatives that society offers. You aren't going to save the day by riding up on your white horse and stopping evil deeds.

The eyes of the public are constantly on the police officer. You are the most visible sign of government, and we all know how people love the government. Law enforcement is one of the few professions that offer twenty-four-hour-a-day responses, seven days a week, including holidays.

You want to become a police officer to help your fellow man? If so, become a social worker, psychologist, or join the Peace Corps. Simply put, your job is to serve and protect. If, for the most part, you want a job that seems thankless and has members of the news media putting your conduct under the microscope, then law enforcement is the career for you.

Another law enforcement officer once told me, "Police officers are like social surgeons. They rid cancer from the body of society." He held his role in society at the same level as that of a skilled surgeon. I carefully thought about what this officer said and realized that, if we work on the body of society, then we must be social proctologists. If you can't figure that out, then law enforcement may not be for you!

If you believe the role of a law enforcement officer is similar to what Hollywood has to offer, then go to Hollywood and get a job in the movies. Hollywood usually shows police officers going into strip bars to deal with bad guys, hookers, and mafia types. I was an active Chicago police officer for over ten years and I never went into a strip bar—not while on duty at least! Get into a shooting in the real world of law enforcement and you will be required to write numerous reports, which Hollywood never shows.

Chances are you will never shoot a human being while on duty as a police officer, but you may be required to shoot a vicious animal. Getting into gun battles is best left to the wizards of Hollywood, and that's a good thing. Some officers are involved in multiple gun battles throughout their careers. Ask them how exciting it was to shoot another human being. Most will answer that they were put in the position to do what they had to do, and it was not glamorous. The power of life and death is at your fingertips, and that's a heavy burden.

Try to understand what the role of a police officer is and whether or not that role is for you. If, by chance, you discover that law enforcement is not a career for you, then get out of it. You won't be doing anyone any favors, including yourself, by staying in a profession that is not of your liking. Remember, you will be required to work assorted shifts in addition to holidays and weekends. This puts stress on you and your family. Any job requires you to spend more conscious hours at that job than you do with anyone else or doing anything else. If you hate your job more than just occasionally, you are in a living hell.

While there is a lot to not like about law enforcement, there is a glimmer of hope that you will really help another human being. Instead of finding the dead, lost child, you find a lost child that's still alive. You may have the opportunity to save someone's life and, if you do so, there is no better feeling. Yes, every once in a while, there is that beautiful rainbow at the end of the storm.

I have seen many individuals try to be a police officer even though they hate the job. There are plenty of things to not like about the law enforcement profession. As a rookie, you will be required to go to the bottom of the list. If someone urinates or vomits in the back of your patrol car, who do you think is going to clean it up? It's not going to be your FTO, your sergeant, your dispatcher, or anyone else. It's you!

You must be tough to be a law enforcement officer. This includes being physically, mentally, and psychologically tough. Tough does not mean being brutal, mean, or having the ability to shut off your emotions under all circumstances. Don't equate being tough with being hard. If you are hard, you are rigid, and you will break. Tough means being like your body armor, which has the ability to bend, yet you can't tear it apart. Being tough protects you, and being *you* allows you to do the job.

Know what is legal, ethical, moral, and correct concerning the law, and your agency's policies, rules, and regulations. Your job is to ensure that citizens have their liberties. When you arrest anyone, you have the power to suspend a citizen's liberty based on the U.S. Constitution and your state's constitution. If you are properly trained as a law enforcement officer, you understand and embrace the power that you have concerning another person's liberty.

Invest the time, money, and effort to be a tough police officer. Think of this as a professional investment. I've seen police officers spend money effortlessly in a bar, yet they will not spend any money on their law enforcement profession. You may need to buy a book and actually read it in order to become a better police officer. There is nothing wrong with spending some of your personal money and time to attend a professional law enforcement training program.

Think of yourself as a member of the "Internet highway patrol" and spend personal time researching various law enforcement and related websites. Be aware that there are numerous websites containing partially true information and misinformation. One website to check wrong information is www.scopes.com, but you can use many professional networking websites to your advantage.

Do not be afraid to assert yourself if you see another officer about to use excessive force. You can save an officer's career or keep that officer from going to prison for criminal behavior. You may not be a supervisor, but you are a law enforcement professional who, above all else, is loyal to the law enforcement profession. In the National Football League, a late hit after the play is over costs 15 yards. A late hit as a law enforcement officer can send you to prison.

It's a good thing to enjoy the professional and social camaraderie that law enforcement can offer. If you work a steady shift along with other officers on a regular basis, it's easy to develop a kindred spirit. This does not mean that members of your shift can do nothing wrong. If you see wrongdoing, it is your sworn duty to right that wrong. As a young officer, you may find it difficult to take formal or even informal steps against a veteran officer. This is why it is important for you to let others know from the start that you are a law enforcement professional with professional standards. If you have never read the "Law Enforcement Code of Ethics," please do so. If you follow this code, you can't go wrong.

Finally, retain your humanity. You are given a tremendous amount of discretion, which means that you can help others, within bounds, by either doing or not doing something. An understanding of the spirit of the law and the letter of the law is important. Remember the difference between being hard and being tough. Perhaps the novelist Agatha Christie said it best, "If one sticks too rigidly to one's principles, one would hardly see anybody." As you know, police officers are required to see everybody.

As always, STAY SAFE!

Ed Nowicki, a retired law enforcement trainer and police officer, is an active law enforcement writer. Ed is authoring a book to be published in 2011, entitled, "American Blue." All royalties from the book will donated to the building of the National Law Enforcement Museum in Washington, DC. Ed can be reached at NCJTC@aol.com.

It's Not About Me

By Brian Willis

I began my career with the Calgary Police Service in 1979 and, when I graduated, I was assigned to 'E' District in downtown Calgary. The police department had not allowed recruits to go from training to the downtown district for a number of years as they felt most recruits were not able to handle what they would face there on a daily basis. That changed with my class and a handful of us were assigned to go downtown. My primary patrol area was the east end of the downtown core. It was the smallest geographic patrol zone in the city but had a high concentration of seedy bars, a lot of drug activity, violence, prostitution and other criminal activity. Just before I graduated, the former commander of that zone took me aside and told me to have a picture taken with all my teeth as I was likely to lose a few early in my career in one of the many fights in which I was sure to find myself. My first thought was that he didn't have confidence in my abilities and I took that personally. However, as I sat back and reflected, I realized "It's not about me." He was simply trying to prepare me for what was to be an eye-opening experience for a 22-year-old rookie. Years later in a promotional interview, I reminded him of the story and we shared a laugh as I smiled to let him know I still had all my teeth.

My first field-training officer hated having to work with me. In fact, he did not talk to me for the first week we worked together. It made for some very long nights, as we were the late care night shift in the district. That meant we started a half hour after everyone else and went home a half hour later in the morning. As an eager young officer, it was hard not to take his resentment of working with me personally. The reality was that "It was not about me." It had to do with a number of factors including having to give up a great long-term partner to work with the new guy. It was about the extra paperwork that comes with being an FTO. It was about the extra responsibility of being an FTO. In a very busy and very violent patrol area, it was also about living with the uncertainty of how your partner was going to react and if he was going to be able to handle himself. It was never about me as a person. By the end of our six weeks together, we had grown to become good friends and learned a great deal from each other.

Early in my career, I had a hard time not taking the insults and verbal and physical attacks personally. Over time, I learned that it was not about me. In fact, it had nothing to do with me personally. It had to do partly with the fact I was a cop, but it was mainly about the other person's rage, biases, anger, fears and other issues. I just happened to be the one that was there to take away their beer, their dope, their spouse or their freedom.

It was harder when victims or people who you were notifying of a death in the family turned on you. Once again, it was not about me. It was about their fears, their anger, their feelings of being violated and their need to lash out at someone or something. I just happened to be the closest target.

The most challenging were times when subjects spit in my face and threatened my family. On one occasion, a subject in the booking area told me he was going to find out where my kids went to school and slit their throats. On the face of it, those are very personal attacks, but it was only about me if I let it be. It was really about the subject trying to piss off the cop that arrested him to get me to say or do something that would come back to haunt me or jeopardize the criminal case.

Over time, I also had to learn not to take internal politics personally. It is easy to get caught up in the moaning, groaning, whining and bitching about "the department," especially when you are the object of an internal investigation. Like everyone else, at times, I got caught up in the, "Woe is me. The agency doesn't care about me"- mindset. Of course, the agency didn't care about me. The agency is just an entity and it is incapable of caring. As Dave Smith says, "Love your job, but don't love your agency because it cannot love you back." In his powerful book, "Emotional Survival for Law Enforcement," Kevin Gilmartin, PhD (2002), reminds us that, "No one will go through their career with their professional virginity intact. Everyone will get screwed by the organization sooner or later." Once we accept that reality, we can prepare for it and deal with it effectively when it happens.

As I progressed through my career and became a trainer, I always had to remember that training was not about me. It is always about the student. As a trainer, no one cares how smart you are or how skilled you are. What they care about is whether you care about them and have the ability to teach them skills that may save their lives. This goes back to one of the key themes of the Excellence in Training course I teach: You have not taught, until they have learned.

In hindsight, I could have saved myself a great deal of stress over the years if I had simply understood this one simple philosophy: It's Not About Me.

As I write this and reflect on the many lessons I have learned over the past 30 years, I have come to realize that as much as it is not about me, it is ALL About Me.

Confused?

Here is what I mean by the statement "It is ALL About Me":

- Being a professional in the face of insults or attacks is a personal choice.
- How I react to politics in the organization is a personal choice.
- Checking my ego at the door as a trainer is a personal choice.

In the end, it is always about choice, and what will help me make a more desirable choice is Life's Most Powerful Question—What's Important Now?

What's Important Now, regarding outside influences and pressures, is to understand "It's not about me."

What's Important Now from a personal perspective it to understand, "It is all about me and the choices I make."

Brian Willis is an internationally recognized thought leader, speaker and trainer drawing on his 25 years of law enforcement experience as a member of the Calgary Police Service over 20 years of training experience to provide cutting edge training to law enforcement officers and trainers throughout North America. Brian operates the innovative training company Winning Mind Training and editor of the highly acclaimed books W.I.N.: Critical Issues in Training and Leading Warriors and W.I.N. 2 Insights Into Training and

Leading Warriors and *If I Knew Then: Life Lessons From Cops on the Street* (www.warriorspiritbooks.com). *Brian serves as the Deputy Executive Director for ILEETA and is a member of NTOA, ITOA, IALEFI, and the Canadian Association of Professional Speakers. Brian can be reached through his website at www.winningmindtraining.com.*

Learning Not to Be Selfish

By David McRoberts

Sometimes what we are taught as small children reappears so often as we grow that we have no choice but to step back and acknowledge how very critical these "life lessons" really are. When pondering the personal meaning of what single thing I wish I had known on day one of police work, that I know all too well now, I had an immediate answer. It is certainly not profound, but it's accurate nevertheless and proven over a 26 year career. Simply stated, what I wish I had known and had a true appreciation for on day one was how nearly every single event, act, and occurrence of tragedy and human suffering that I experienced on the job had at its foundation a behavioral trait that we are were cautioned about and against as young children: *selfishness*. It's that simple.

Initially, it's not easy to understand the association, but it becomes simple in its correlation over time—once you "connect the dots." At first glimpse, this seems overly simplistic, but it's this short and simple truth of a person only thinking about themselves, without regard for the sacrifice or suffering of others, that really cuts to the core of the issue. Selfishness is the central theme for nearly all of the misery that law enforcement is called upon to mediate, resolve, and intercede, or more often just plain clean up. People who are only concerning themselves with what they want, when they want it, and not caring about anyone else, is all too pervasive in the lives of many with whom law enforcement must interact daily. The list can be a long one and reads like a criminal code statute book: trespassing, burglary, theft, battery, domestic abuse, sexual abuse, drunk driving, child abuse and neglect, elder abuse and neglect, extortion, stalking, corruption, and homicide all have at their core this most debilitating trait of selfishness... "me first and the hell with anyone else."

Personal and all too often *immediate* gratification, to the exclusion of any and all concern about who we interact and associate with, plays itself out every day. None of us is immune. When considering this point there are many other destructive human emotions that surface. Jealousy and envy jump to mind. Both are at best counterproductive, and at worst destructive. When thought of carefully, these two additional detriments have, at their core, selfishness as a building block.

The brutal reality is that we have all suffered from bouts of selfishness as we move through our lives that have diminished us. I believe that working every day not to succumb to the debilitating affect of this destructive force is the only way to defeat it. I accepted the fact that as a law enforcement officer I would encounter the full gamut of behaviors that comprise a day of patrol work in the field. From the noncompliance of habitual offenders, to the self-medicating abusers of alcohol and drugs, right up to the various forms of violence that are acted out in homes, schools, and workplaces every day, I believe that each destructive activity can be traced back to the core behavior of selfishness. We have to neutralize this whenever we can.

The crimes of burglary and theft are the easiest to associate with the behavior of being selfish: permanently taking something that does not belong to you without permission. Seems simple enough, but wait—is it really? What are the most basic reasons that this "stealing" occurred? The reasons are clear to me now after years of dealing with those that victimize others in this way. They want something they are either not entitled to or worked to get without the effort that someone else expended to acquire it appropriately. Taking what you want without regard for the owner or anyone else just because you want it or feel you are entitled to it—selfish by definition. Didn't we ever learn this lesson as kids? When we were kids, we were corrected for taking toys from others that weren't ours. We were reprimanded as adolescents for conveniently taking a book, make-up, or some change from the locker or purse of a "friend" when their back was turned. We were admonished as young adults for driving recklessly, underage drinking, or moving too quickly in a moment of closeness on a date where the words "no" and "stop" didn't register. It all comes down to satisfying our own needs first and foremost with no consideration for others.

From my first day on the only job I ever wanted, right up to my retirement party, the destructive human trait of selfishness accounted for the greatest percentage of reactive effort expended by the proud men and women I worked with every day. Acts of ultimate selfishness by others even took the lives of two of them, leaving voids where friends, fathers, and husbands once stood. Even as I took my oath to serve and protect on my first day on the job, I accepted the fact that I couldn't solve everything or save everyone. As a young and imperfect man myself, I understood the shortcomings of the citizens I had sworn to protect, I just really never connected the most easily understood lessons taught as a child to the almost unspeakable events which I would respond and react to in my career. I just wish I could have identified this simple truth sooner in my career—so many things would have made more sense. Maybe I would have had a much clearer understanding of the sometimes-incomprehensible events that my colleagues and I had to witness.

Now, for the record, we in police work are granted no special exemption from this debilitating behavior. We are human and we are not perfect. Less than stellar behavior plays out each and every day on the job as well. Yes, it is much better controlled and managed by professional peacekeepers within the structure and discipline of our agencies; but it is still deadly to attitudes, interest, and initiative for every department member. The petty jealously of special treatment and training offerings, the envy of special assignments and promotional selections, the selfishness of not acknowledging effort, results, and recognition where deserved. Any one of us with enough time on the job knows these things exist. We owe it each other to fight to learn the lessons and eliminate this internal strife.

You learn these things early in life. My grandmother used to recite the following lesson for me: "If you lie, you will cheat; if you cheat, you will steal; and if you steal you can commit murder." Now that was some very heavy-handed old school philosophy from two generations past. Not much room for misinterpretation in that lesson. In my estimation the expression and actions of selfishness are woven through that one-sentence lesson tightly, and knotted at the end by the word *murder*, so its message never becomes unraveled, misunderstood, or otherwise minimized. I often wondered where she heard it from initially. Regardless of the source, it couldn't be more accurate in its description of the erosion and destruction of core values and traits by selfishness.

I heard the lesson often as I grew up. The last time I heard it she was delivering it to my brother on the day before she was murdered. That same kind of erosion of values came to the breaking point for my only brother who was being consumed by hate, hopelessness, drugs, and selfishness, and stabbed our grandmother to death—one of the last people on this earth that was still trying to help him. I think it's very clear that he never heard her message or learned the lesson.

I know, I know, I know... It just seems too simple that selfishness is at the core of all this destruction; but does something have to be complicated to make sense? I don't think so. I only wish I had gotten a better handle on the depths of its meaning when I first started my career. Maybe, then, this core of senseless human suffering would have been better understood or at least better anticipated... because for me, from a most personal perspective, it will never make any sense.

If I only knew then what I know all too well now; if you learn nothing else in life, take any and all steps necessary to avoid becoming a selfish person and the rest of your life just might fall into place less painfully, with a greater degree of satisfaction and serenity.

Stay safe.

David W. McRoberts is the Vice President of Business Development for L.R. Kimball, an architectural firm that designs Law Enforcement and Justice Facilities nationwide. Prior to joining Kimball, Mr. McRoberts served on the Kenosha County Wisconsin Sheriff's Department, retiring as a Captain in 2002. David is a member of the Advisory Board for ILEETA. He has three children, four grandchildren, and lives within State College, Pennsylvania, with his wife Debbie.

Life is a Precious Gift

By Vince O'Neill

This is a true story. Only the names have been changed to protect the innocent. Just two weeks ago, a friend and colleague called to report that John Wane, whom I've known for a considerable time, took his own life. The hard drive kicked in, as some twenty years of memories flashed by my heads-up screen. I said something. What, I have no clue. But I was searching for words. *That*, I remember. You see, in my thirty-six years of law enforcement, this was the third such incident to touch me. No matter how immune one might think he or she is to such happenings, all the homicides, multi-fatality accidents, medical emergencies, SIDS cases, and, yes, suicides, it's still a shock when it happens to one of our own. What I heard from John's coworkers, friends, and family was, "He's the last person in the world I would have suspected of doing something like this." You mean suicide? Yes! Suicide! I felt that hardness coming over me.

John graduated from the state academy in the winter of 1991. He was filled with enthusiasm, excitement, and wonder. (You trainers know of whom I speak.) John bought into the vernacular, "You can be on God's green earth for a thousand years, and you ain't gonna learn it all up. But you sure as hell can try. At the end of thirty years, you may have even forgotten 99 percent of what you learned, but the one percent you've retained will be like a thousand percent over-and-beyond the average natural endowment of the human race. We call it savvy!" And John was a savvy kind of guy. He never held anything back; he gave it his all; he was, in a word, a "perfectionist." He was physically gifted, mentally astute, and spiritually straight. It was a real pleasure to have him in class.

Just a few years later, John showed up for a CLEET's four-week Defensive Tactics Instructor School by the Council on Law Enforcement Education and Training (CLEET). Not a give-away- certification by any means. Every DTI candidate went through rigorous physical skills training in many areas of the art. They learned how to fall and recover. They learned relative positioning and how to "combat dance," i.e., patterns of movement. All candidates were exposed to a plethora of open-hand techniques, as well as the really fun stuff, like

- Gary Klugiewicz's active counter-measures program, counter-choke take-downs and escapes, ground tactics;
- Jim Lindell's and Grav Maga's weapon retention/disarming techniques, knife/counter-knife ;
- John Boren's Universal Baton (Petiki Tersia Arnis);
- Lon Anderson's PR-24;
- Dennis Orcutt's Police Nunhaku, Biradial takes-downs, Controlled FORCE mechanical advantage holds, OC Counter Assault and Survival Tactics (the first of its kind in the United States);
- The Oklahoma Universal Restraint (OUR) Handcuffing System, RIPP Restraints, and open-hand/impact weapon assisted car extractions, and more.

The "software" included Management of Aggressive Behavior, harnessing Neuro-Linguistic Programming as a teaching tool, Use of Force Options (UFO) Matrices, Medical Implications, combat physiology, post violent event trauma, and UFO Reporting Systems. John was at the top of his class.

John was a *natural* teacher. That is to say, he loved teaching Defensive Tactics, Custody Control, and Use of Force Options. His intensity and ready smile were infectious. The student's caught on. Everyone knew what the smile meant. He was, quite frankly, one of our best.

Years go by so quickly, it seems like a big blur sometimes. Yet, when we reflect on where we've been and where we're going, time seems to come down to being a matter of opposites, relatively speaking. It seems like yesterday that John was assisting me with a basic academy class, yet, it seems so yesteryear at the same time; like one minute my baby boy was born, then, the next minute his mother and I are waiting for him to come back home from the war in Iraq. That kind of dichotomy. All of that passed through my mind as I heard the news of John Wane's passing. Thoughts of, "Was there something I could have done to prevent this? Was there something I could have said to change his mind? Was I careless? How come I didn't pick up on this?"

Well, we get a lot of education on what to look and listen for, etc., but we never really know how this process works out all of the time. What I know now that I didn't know then is that there is a great amount of ambivalence and turmoil in the pre-suicidal decision. You see, suicide is a gamble. Suicidal officers are very conscious of the risk factor; they tempt fate to see if life or death will win out. The problem, of course, is that when an officer commits suicide, there is commonly the failure to not only to see that he wanted to die, but that he also wanted to live. Yet, for some people, there is no ambivalence at all: they simply want to die, and there's nothing anyone can do to prevent their death once the decision had has been made. But these people are the exception. Most want to live *and* to die. In the former, there is hope.

What I knew before, but forgot, is that there are several different types of motivation for suicide, and all of them are tied to ways one sees himself relative to his place in society. There are anomic, egoistic, manipulative and surcease suicides. *Anomic* suicide is usually precipitated by a shattering break in an officer's relationship to his society: economic depression, loss of job, sudden wealth, or even sudden promotion. *Egoistic* motivations occur when the officer has too few ties to his fellow human beings. The presupposition to live no longer exists in the egoistic mode. Some officers wish to *manipulate* the remainder of their world by dying: to have the final word in an argument, revenge against a rejecting lover or divorcing spouse; to ruin the life of another person. And then, there are those who wish to *surcease*. They've simply given up. Their emotional distress is intolerable; they see no alternative solution to their problems. *Émouvoir* notwithstanding, they see death as the end to their problems by embracing nothingness in perpetual sleep. Finally, there is the *altruistic* suicide, which, as it happens, seldom involves police officers. That said, society at large seems to be turning toward euthanasia as baby-boomers get older. Altruistic suicide is required by society, in order that the community might benefit. Hara-kiri, for instance, is a form of altruistic self-extermination. Contemporary discussion of Death Panels may portend a socially acceptable form of altruistic suicide. Understand, though, suicide is a permanent solution to a temporary problem. If there's anything in the way of neutralizing presuppositions relevant to life and death, this is it. Then, of course, there are combinations.

It's no secret that police officers have one of the highest divorce rates in the country. They also have twice the suicide rate of "average Americans," anywhere from ten 10 to 16.34 per 100,000. The ecology of a police officer's mind can get fairly toxic after a while, especially when no one seems to be paying attention. Add to the latter extensively altered presuppositions and worldview, and, well, life can, more often than not, become meaningless without a workable moral compass.

As I understand it, John's wife had just left him after nearly 19 years of marriage. He had five children, two from his wife's previous marriage and three of their own. He had just been promoted to Chief of Police and; he was a great COP (Certified Official Peacekeeper). His officers respected him; he was a loving father and husband; a loyal friend; and he was involved with his community and in his church's youth ministry. He was a father figure to the many young people he came into contact with, and he was even respected by the offenders he fought and arrested. By all accounts, life was good. The news of his demise was devastating. It rocked the community to its core.

Life is a precious gift. But no one knew of the dark place in John's life. Not even his closest friends. He went into the Stygian, the River Styx, never to return. A good man, he was said to be an "all or nothing at all" kind of guy. This was the sort of mindset that endeared him to many of his colleagues. John always gave it his all. And perhaps, that's how he chose to conclude his time on earth: all or nothing at all. So, he gave it *all* up. Could we have pulled him back from the Grim Reaper? I don't know. But I know this: all three of my friends who chose to end it all were decorated war veterans. As law enforcement officers, they were over-achievers. They were defensive tactics and firearms instructors; they had high expectations of themselves and others; they were competitive; they were perfectionists; they were loved, respected, and admired; and they were the last people on God's green earth you would have ever expected to commit suicide. I submit, the latter is but another indicator. Perhaps we overlook the obvious sometimes. Now *you know now* before it becomes —"if I knew *then*." If I knew then what I know now, I could have done a better job of allaying doubts and fears of my brother and sister officers—putting things in perspective.

Strategies? Yes. Brian Willis's program, "What's Important Now," or W.I.N., as it's commonly known, can go a long way towards resolving such inner conflict. If we make W.I.N. part of our personalities, now practice it at least 33 times a day, and the fight down the road, whether it's on the street or in our personal lives, won't seem as onerous. Hopelessness, apathy, and willful self-deception, after all, are the antithesis of W.I.N. Like baking a cake, when you eat some of the raw ingredients, by themselves like flour, baking powder, milk, salt, sugar, raw eggs, peanut oil, vanilla, one at a time, or all at once—the way life throws it at you sometimes—for most people, just the thought of it can almost make them sick. Then, again, once it's all mixed up, stick it in the oven, bake it, then cool and ice it, well, you might find that life, er, cake, is really pretty good. Lastly, that voiceless voice that whispers deep inside your very being? Listen to it. That's God talking to you. Don't underestimate the power of prayer. The "*hole*," wherever it is, is a lonely place. Some of you know that. Share your experiences. Peace.

Vince O'Neill has over 35 years of law enforcement experience and is currently serving as the Senior Staff Instructor and Firearms Training Coordinator at the Oklahoma Council on Law Enforcement Education and Training. After sixteen 16 years with the Lawrence, Kansas Police Department, serving in many capacities, Vince was recruited by John Boren, the legendary Defensive Tactics (DT) coordinator of the Oklahoma CLEET. O'Neill took over as DT Coordinator when

Boren moved to New Mexico State Police Academy in 1991 as Bureau Chief. O'Neill was certified a Monadnock PR-24 International Instructor Trainer, certified by the late, great Lon Anderson and the ever-moving Terry Smith.

A leading innovator while on the national staff of the National Law Enforcement Training Center, and a championship shooter, he has made his presence felt at such venues as LFI, H&K, and has certified Smith & Wesson's national training staff in weapon retention/disarming tactics just to name a few. He continues to teach DT and firearms at the national level and enjoys being assigned to Mas Ayoob's Panel of Experts at ILEETA training seminars.

Vince was a major contributor to ASLET, in its heyday, delivering eleven presentations in as many years. He has trained officers from all fifty states, and several European jurisdictions. Vince is certified as an expert witness in the federal system, and continues to serve in that capacity. He's among the strongest supporters of Brian Willis's W.I.N. Program. His favorite quotes are: "The nation that makes a great distinction between its scholars and its warriors will have its thinking done by cowards and its fighting done by fools. The State that separates its scholars from its warriors will have its thinking done by cowards and its fighting done by fools" (Thucydides) and, "In Hoc Signo Vinces," meaning "With this as your standard you shall have victory. By this sign you shall conquer."

Nothing is Forever

By Guy Rossi

I was fortunate to have retired from my career in law enforcement over 12 years ago. Like many of my peers, I didn't retire because of trials of the street, but instead because a high-ranking supervisor told me I was going to be taking on an impossible assignment of "doing more with less." At the time, I was overseeing the Field and Recruit Training Unit of a large metropolitan agency in New York. I loved being involved in training new blood and took pride when the unexpected recruit blossomed into a street-smart officer. I retired with just about every national and state certification available in officer survival, defensive tactics, and instructor development for law enforcement. I thought that transferring my skills over to the private sector would be an easy jump...wrong!

Four months later, I was offered a job by our regional academy overseeing police in-service training. Essentially, I became the extension of my previous job as a civilian and, instead of doing it for one department, I was doing it for the entire county and the six county regions bordering our county. I was lucky and, ironically, it was as though I never left the job as I worked alongside the same people I had left at the P.D. The only difference was a larger scope of responsibilities and I no longer had to carry a gun! Life was good and I had the best of both worlds.

Someone once told me that, regardless of how important we feel we are to a group, or profession in this case, once we leave the group our accomplishments will soon be forgotten. Although such comments made sense, one seldom believes it will apply to them.

I remember one time sitting in a meeting, discussing the curriculum development and schedule for the next police recruit class. In the meeting were training officers from the academy and regional police departments as well as from the agency from which I retired four months earlier. We began discussing the new changes in defensive tactics that would have to be trained to the field-training officers before the recruits hit the street, so that they were evaluated appropriately. Having been the prior supervisor of field training for the largest agency in the area as well as personally instructing the Field Training Officer School for several years, I believed that my presence and opinion would be solicited from those who now carried the torch. Wrong! I was stunned as my prior subordinates disregarded my helpful suggestions. When I spoke on the subject, no one listened. I realized that what I said no longer held any weight because I was not speaking from a position of authority. My perception was that they no longer regarded me as a subject matter expert in the topic. I felt like someone had taken a pin and exploded my ego balloon. Again, I was wrong. What I had failed to do was realize that the trainers would not react to the authority I once held; however, I needed to now appeal to logic, research, and proven methodologies that were timely and factual. It took me several years to realize that although I was still a part of the culture of active police officers, I was now on the periphery. No longer a bird of the same feather, I would have to appeal to them in a different manner than I was once accustomed.

People often joke that when you step away from any group you will become the target of their ridicule. It took me nearly 10 years to come to terms that once you leave the fold it will be as if you were never there. The most important lesson to retain from this is that all of your accomplishments and "war stories" will soon be forgotten. When you leave the job, what you will be remembered for is how you treated people. The label of being an accomplished trainer, fearless police officer, etc., will soon erode with time. The best accomplishment is to walk by a group of rookies and, when one asks the other about you, they say something like, "Yeah he was on the job—he's a good guy."

Guy Rossi is a retired Police Sergeant of the Rochester, New York, Police Department who specialized in patrol, recruit, field training, and defensive tactics instruction. He has been a nationally recognized law enforcement trainer since 1982. His experiences in officer survival skills have been published in over two hundred magazine articles and chapters in books on training. Upon retiring from active duty, he was employed as a Program Coordinator of Curriculum Development for the Public Safety Training Facility of Monroe Community College (MCC). Presently he is a Program Coordinator of Curriculum Development for the Homeland Security Management Institute of MCC. Guy has a Master's Degree in Adult Education—Instructional Design. He is also a proud charter member of the International Law Enforcement and Educators Training Association (ILEETA) and serves as the Editor of the prestigious ILEETA Review. In his spare time, Guy continues to peck away at law enforcement training-related articles as well as a serial killer novel he has been working on entitled, "Bloodline."

On Weakness and Strength

By Jack Colwell

If fifty-year-old Jack Colwell could go back in time and talk to twenty-one year old Jack Colwell, just before he enters the Academy, this is what he would say:

You are a young idealistic person. Get ready: your childhood memories of "Adam-12" as your mental portrayal of police work are about to be shattered. What cops are like, how they talk to each other and how they respond to members of our community are like a sweet dream you are about to be rudely awakened from. You have not been a particularly good kid, but you have never heard so many expletives and hostile labels crammed into short dialogue quips. Your first ride along will be both scary and exhilarating. It will set you on a course of increasing confusion. You will learn to interpret warning signs of weakness as strengths. I am a seasoned veteran now, talking to you after over twenty-eight years of service. I do not claim to have obtained wisdom; I have only finally learned to desire humility. By the way, Jack, I am also talking to our son, who at fifteen has his heart set on being a cop—each of you, please seriously consider these thoughts.

Self-righteous indignation will make you feel strong but it brutalizes your soul, destroys relationships, and renders you devoid of influence.

On the job, you will see many things that will incite a sense of self-righteous indignation in you. People will have lifestyles that you will find repugnant and make decisions you will find hilarious. You and your friends on the job will be tempted to make sport of them and will naturally reach ever-increasing heights of indignation. You will feel completely justified in your indignation—in fact, you will see no alternative. This indignation will feel so right and good but it is poison to your soul; it kills relationships and decimates your influence. Indignation slays humility because the two are mutually exclusive. Indignation crushes patience and renders wisdom impossible. You will begin to see people as bits and pieces of a meaningless puzzle. You will not care enough to put the pieces together and you will fall into cynicism.

> Humility will make you feel weak but it builds character, nourishes relationships, and releases influence.

Influence is the most important resource for cops. I estimate that during an average workday, there are approximately 6000 people in our city for each on-duty officer! Influence creates and sustains a cooperative bond that increases law enforcement effectiveness by order of magnitude.

With humility, you will see the lifestyles and choices of others as a reminder of your own weaknesses and compromises. Then you can look at others with compassion, not judgment. With compassion, you can accomplish impartial service to the Law, rather than mindless enforcement of laws. This is the basis of true justice.

Compassion combined with a strong sense of justice will allow you to make difficult decisions and take hard actions while upholding the nobility of our profession. Compassion and justice are a soothing balm to hurting and confused people. Combined—humility, compassion, justice, nobility, and the resulting wisdom are inspirational and contagious—they are superpowers! You will gain real insight into complex problems and uncover the simplicity of the root causes. Your problem solving skills will seem phenomenal, but they will simply be a reflection of the collective wisdom inspired around you. You will become a centrifuge of influence, cooperation, and effectiveness. There may never be the one big event that grabs lots of attention and notoriety. Your influence will be more like a still, small voice, instilling integrity, courage, patience, and wisdom in others. This will create synergy that will scatter attention away from you, producing a solar system with an almost invisible sun at the center. You will not be lauded, maybe not even noticed, but you will have an inner peace and joy that far surpasses all the momentary accolades.

I know this is possible, because I have seen a precious few who live this out. I will not say who they are because they do not want the attention—they are too busy caring for people, leading with vision and instilling true justice into their community. That is what I wish for you.

Jack L. Colwell is the co-author, along with Charles Huth, of Unleashing the Power of Unconditional Respect: Transforming Law Enforcement and Police Training *(2010). He is the cofounder and co-instructor of the Regional Police Academy, Leadership Academy for the Kansas City, Missouri, Police Department, where he has served for over twenty-eight years. His duties have included patrol, tactical, investigations, primary and secondary education, and professional, leadership, and organizational development. Jack holds numerous nationally recognized leadership and personal development content certifications. He is a recent graduate of the U.S. Army's University of Foreign Military and Cultural Studies (UFMCS, in Fort Leavenworth, Kansas) Red Team Member's Course 09-004. He has created and implemented several successful training processes and initiatives. Jack is on the advisory board for the Vatterott College Criminal Justice Program in St. Joseph, Missouri, and holds a Bachelor of Science degree from the Baptist College of Florida. He resides in Kansas City, Missouri, with his wife of twenty-nine years, Sherri. Sherri and Jack have five children, two of whom are married (with two grandchildren on the way). Blog: http://unleashingrespect.blogspot.com; e-mail: unleashingrespect@gmail.com.*

Reader Writer Thinker Fighter: The Way of Ronin

By Bill Westfall

Ask any young police officer what their primary role is and so many will reply, "I'm a crime fighter, I'm here to put the bad guy in jail." Many of us probably said the same thing when we were at that stage of our law enforcement careers. But in time, most of us realized that the "fighter" part of the job is only a small part of the police officer's role and, in time, wisdom teaches us that we prefer that confrontation be minimized, when possible.

European police administrators, when asked about the primary role of police officers in their society, normally respond, "It is to educate the public about the law, and one of the tools we have is arrest." In their systems and their training, they reinforce this concept, role, and definition. It is proactive in their mindset. American society and American policing does differ from our European counterparts. We are a more violent society. And, yes, officers everywhere will always have to be fighters, and they should be highly skilled and properly prepared in those areas so that violent incidents can be minimized and handled as safely as possible for all those concerned. But maybe the time has come for this generation of law enforcement leadership to offer an improved definition other that of "fighter."

The Way of Ronin

The way of the Ronin (pronounced ROHW-NIN,) is derived from a unique kind of warrior who emerged in Japan following the feudal period. They were Samurai separated from their feudal lords by choice or as a result of getting caught in a power struggle or crossfire. They emerged as independents becoming their own masters that could not be leveraged by either the war or feudal lords. Ronin means literally, "the wave people" who ride, anticipate, and even make waves of change on their own.

The Ronin's activities are steered by professional growth and fueled by their own passion for their profession. Ronins are not hired guns or rogues. Ronins are fueled by their commitment to some calling, vocation, or mission, and are loyal to their cause and their organization, truly serving its mission. They realize that their true "legacy" is the result of organizational, individual, and personal growth. They are also loyal to their fellow Ronins involved in that cause. Because they are committed to a mission with meaning, and they have passion for that mission, they are feared by those who are simply hired guns following a money trail. Such Samurai know the Ronin cannot be leveraged, compromised, or tempted by offerings of power, influence, position, or promises of riches. As a result, they will sometimes be feared, sometimes isolated and, unless Ronins develop extraordinary diplomatic and statesman-like skills, in time an attempt will be made to ease or force them out.

To do Ronin, one must have a depth in basic skills. Just as the Ronin of old had to be a skilled warriors in the basics so must the Ronin of today. The Ronin of today must be more than fighter; they must be Reader, Writer, Thinker, Fighter. Ronins today must have extraordinary basic skills, honed and steeled to an exceptional level. They must be disciplined self-managers, have the ability to "quick study," have exceptional speaking and writing skills, and must know how to nurture team building and team playing. This foundation of basic skills will then support a career path fueled by the passion of their mission that will develop into unique expertise. The basic philosophy of the Ronin is a commitment to a life-long quest of helping people to achieve their full potential through nurtured learning and peak performance.

Application of Ronin: Reader, Writer, Thinker, Fighter: The Lesson of Aguda.

David Hackworth was the most decorated living American warrior of our lifetime until his untimely death in 2005. He holds two distinguished service crosses (the only higher award is a Medal of Honor), ten silver stars, eight bronze stars, and eight purple hearts. Many of you saw him on television talk shows. Silver-gray hair, black turtlenecks, he was usually invited to such programs by the conservatives, but he owed his soul to no one. He was always forthright, spoke his mind and with the "bark on." He spoke on behalf of the individual fighting soldier. He called them Willie Lump Lump.

In the prime of his career as a full colonel who was destined for at least two and maybe three stars, he resigned his commission in protest not of the Vietnam War itself, but of the manner in which the war was being fought. He did soon appeared on national TV stating that "he can could no longer ask young men to die for a cause that he realized the military leadership was not committed to winning," and could not win given their delusionary strategy and tactics.

There are many lessons in the life and odyssey of this American Warrior. A fifteen 15-year-old semi-orphaned school dropout who hedged about his age to enlist in the U.S. Army, Hackworth found himself in Europe in 1945 shortly before the end of the Second World War. Finding a home for the first time in his life, this impressionable fifteen year old was "written on" by the finest army this country had fielded with the possible exception of the 1991 and current Middle East wars. For those who trained and mentored him, had survived years and months of war and were masters of their trade.

At the age of eighteen, he found himself in Korea, and promptly went AWOL from his infantry company because they were not committed to fighting. Promoted to sergeant and later field commissioned to lieutenant, Hackworth left Korea as a 201-year-old captain. He had led a ranger company that spent most of its time behind the lines of the enemy. Sitting in a San Francisco bar as a young captain and recipient of a distinguished service cross, two silver stars, three bronze stars, and three purple hearts he was arrested by MPs for impersonating an officer.

It was about this time that Hackworth realized that his army career would be stifled unless he overcame his inability to write. Although an accomplished warrior, he realized that the army was changing and that he was a one-dimensional warrior.

Hackworth went on to finish high school and complete both undergraduate and graduate degrees, and authored a Vietnam primer that was issued to infantrymen when they arrived in Vietnam. This orphaned high school drop out later co-authored and authored numerous professional articles and a number of books. He became the Reader, Writer, Thinker, Fighter and learned the Way of Ronin.

This did not come easy for him. But his realization of a changing army coupled with an experience he had as a young sergeant in Korea convinced him of the need to become the Reader, Writer, Thinker, Fighter.

Hackworth's company had been given a mission of relieving a beleaguered infantry company on a hill called Logan. The company had been overrun the night before. They had taken heavy casualties and were expecting an early morning counteroffensive by Chinese regulars in the early morning hours.

As Hackworth's company moved on line, they began to take small arms fire. The hill was, like so many in Korea, poor footing, steep slopes full of pits and rough terrain. In such a situation, it is imperative that small arms and especially automatic weapons get online, so that a base of fire can be laid down to dissuade concentration of small arms fire on any one portion of the line.

There was a huge Hawaiian in Hackworth's company in a neighboring platoon by the name of Aguda. Aguda's weapon was a Browning Automatic Rifle (BAR), or automatic rifle; one of those weapons so crucial to the success of the morning defense. Hackworth loved and respected Aguda for his emotional battle personality. He was a warrior's warrior. As Aguda settled into position, he had to often rise up from his position of cover and expose himself and his position in order to lay down, the all-important base of fire. As he would do so, he would, of course, draw fire. Each time he did so it allowed a few more men to get on line from both his platoon as well as Hackworth's group. Each time he would expose himself in order to fire, they would yell at him to, "Get down! Get down!" They were fearful he would be hit. Each time he would raise up the small arms fire would get closer and more concentrated. Finally, everyone within sight saw that Aguda had been hit. Rather than just lie there and call out for aid, he repositioned himself and began once again returning fire. First a superficial wound and then they saw his body rack from more severe wounds and finally in both resignation and disregard for his own welfare he simply stood up concentrating his fire on the approaching enemy. Of course, when he did so the opposing line erupted and, in time, Aguda, fell to his knees still firing, and then slumped over, no longer moving. Aguda had sacrificed himself at a crucial time in the defense of that hill. Many that were struggling to get into position were able to do so when the enemy concentrated their firepower on silencing Aguda's relentless defense.

Hackworth, saddened by the death of this behemoth of a warrior was resigned that Aguda's death should not go unrecognized. When his platoon returned to reserve status, it was the time given to replenishing their supplies and to reflect on those who made a difference in the recent battle. It was here that the deeds of those who had made a difference would be recognized by nominations for awards. It was unusual that for nominations to come from someone outside of the nominee's other than from those within the same platoon. But Hackworth, determined that Aguda's sacrifice would not go unheralded, lead the initiative to recognize his friend.

Now listen to his commentary, for it is here that the analogy to our own profession is so clear. He said, "We were a bunch of ignorant kids from the wrong side of the tracks. Most of us had grown up in poor homes." They were a microcosm of America; there were African American, Anglos, Chicano, and Latinos. "Dispensable rainbows," he called them. "Some of us could barely read and write. We didn't have time for that sissy stuff. We were fighters not writers." So those ignorant, dispensable rainbows tore the top off an old C-ration box and, as best they could, began to write their nomination:

> "Aguda was a good man.
> Aguda killed a lot of the enemy.
> Aguda saved our ass up on Logan.
> He deserves the Big One, the Blue Max,
> the Medal of Honor."

So, in four simple and somewhat vague sentences, these ignorant, unsophisticated, naive, "dispensable rainbows," made a recommendation for a Medal of Honor. It is elegant in its own way, albeit, crude, and simplistic. If you were there, it somehow works. But what if you weren't there? Little vague, wouldn't you say? It didn't talk about how critical Aguda was to the defense of Logan. It didn't describe how he was wounded, not once, but three times, and yet he kept returning fire. Of course, the recommendation went to the rear to an educated, sophisticated captain in a nice warm tent who reviewed the nomination. In reflection, Hackworth realized this educated captain, in the nice warm tent probably said to him self, "Well we're all good men or we wouldn't be here. We all kill a lot of the enemy and save lives by doing so, ummm… Silver Star."

While eloquent to those young warriors present during Aguda's heroism, the nomination fell short once presented to an audience who was out of touch with their battlefield. It was just too vague. Although disappointed, Hackworth didn't get angry at with the captain. He realized he owned a part of this failure. Simply because Hackworth and his well intended group didn't know how to spell it, didn't know how to say it, a very brave, a very deserving warrior had gone unrecognized. He began to understand how important it was for a leader to be able to write and articulate an argument. He made himself a promise that, he would get an education and never again would one of his deserving warriors go unrecognized because he simply did not know how to say it. It was then that Hackworth vowed that he would learn how to spell, how to write, and how to say it. You see, he recognized that no one can tell the story; no one can explain the need like the warrior himself, who is immersed first hand in the battle.

Hackworth's first book, "About Face: The Odyssey of an American Warrior," (1990), was nearly 900 pages in length. He has written or co-authored at least two more that I know of. He co-authored a "how to" manual to fight the war in Vietnam. Sadly, the powers to be didn't read it.

I wrote him twice. I wrote to thank him for his first book. It helped me to understand our strategic, tactical, and political failures in Vietnam. In both instances, he wrote back. Given how busy he was, I was as always amazed he responded. Let's see if he learned to write.

> *Dear Bill:*
> *Your beautiful letter, alone, made the now seven-year journey of writing and touring on behalf of About Face, worth the entire effort.*
>
> *The writing of About Face chased a lot of devils from my head.*
>
> *Suggest you write a piece for Vietnam magazine there in Leesburg. They need articles from warriors rather than the "white wash clerks" that write for them now.*
>
> *Semper Fi, Hack*

Notice the first paragraph. He thanks me? He makes me feel better about who I am as a person; something all great leaders do. The second paragraph he shares something personal. Another reason I liked his book, as a Vietnam Veteran, the book chased a lot of devils from my head as well. The third paragraph infers, "Now, don't you just sit there; do something to make a difference as well." Leaders always encourage others to make a difference. And then he signs the letter, Semper Fi, Hack. A career Army officer acknowledges the former Marine.

We're fighters not writers. Does this sound familiar? Don't we see ourselves as more fighters than writers? As I move around the country and interact with law enforcement administrators, from time-to-time we will be asked to write policy and procedure. We rarely do. There is a specific reason: No one can tell your story; no one quite knows your jurisdiction—your jurisdiction's culture—like those who work there day-to-day. Oh, we can help with resources, make recommendations based on generic principles, but the gut-wrenching writing that will provide meaningful procedure to that first-line officer is from those who know and understand their jurisdiction and only them.

Until we learn how to write, how to say it, how to diplomatically state it diplomatically, with statesman-like clarity, not the public, not the courts, not the prosecutor, not and even our administration will not understand it. How many officers have been failed by vague, poorly written policy and procedures? How many deserving criminals have gone unpunished simply because an officer didn't understand the need or have the skills to properly execute their roles, not as fighter, but as Reader, Writer, Thinker, Fighter? How many more generations of police will continue to fail due to an ill-defined role as only fighter?

We keep waiting for the media, television, and movies to tell our story. They won't because they can't. One of the great unknowns in this country is the quality of our people; people who are willing to risk and even give their life lives for people they don't even know. The public doesn't realize that it because the only stories they will hear from the media are the ones that generally embarrass or humiliate the profession. Only we can tell our story.

One of my first supervisors, a corporal by the name of Don Lawrence used to return my reports with so much red ink on them they looked like somebody had hemorrhaged on them. I would turn in two and get back FOUR. The first year, I grew to dislike him and his damnable red pen. But, in time, I learned to respect him and even later to admire and care for him. You see, he was concerned enough about my individual growth that he could subjugate his own ego need for acceptance in order for me to eventually grow. In time, I learned to write a report that was concise, clearly written, that contained all elements of the crime, and could be used by a prosecutor. He did me a great favor. His efforts contributed to a legacy that sustained itself long after he left the police service.

Someone once said that leaders who nurture and mentor their charges and develop them to their full potential are, "creating living messages for a time they will not see." All of us are doing that now. What is the message, the legacy this generation of police leadership will leave? That of fighter, or that of Ronin, The Reader, Writer, Thinker, Fighter?

I loved David Hackworth for the way he cared for, respected, protected, and spoke on behalf of "Willy Lump, Lump." He was the essence of Ronin. David Hackworth died in May of 2005 of cancer, believed to be related to exposure to

Agent Orange and Agent Blue. I was taken aback by his unexpected, untimely, and premature death. He was bigger than life to me, a true American Hero, and his was a voice that will not only be missed, but also, in my estimation, will never be replaced. I knew he couldn't, but somehow, I thought he would live forever. He will be in my heart and mind and in the hearts and minds of all the "Willy Lump Lumps."

Semper Fi, Hack! He was the essence of Reader, Writer, Thinker, Fighter.

William S. Westfall is currently President of the Gallagher, Westfall Group of Indiana, where he manages, develops, and provides a wide range of leadership, supervision, and management services to the public sector. He has provided, liability, leadership, and supervisory training to thousands of police officers and public sector personnel in nearly every state in the United States. He has also been featured as a guest speaker on the Law Enforcement Television Network (LETN), the Fire Emergency Television Network (FETN), The University of Portsmouth, England, General Session Speaker for the 1997 ASLET Conference and the 2006 ILEETA conference. He is well known for practical but powerful motivational and inspirational learning experiences.

Mr. Westfall served previously as Deputy Director of the Institute for Liability Management providing training and support to law enforcement administrators, risk managers, and self-insured pools to reduce law enforcement, criminal justice, and public safety liability.

Prior to his appointment with the Institute, Mr. Westfall was Director of the Montana Law Enforcement Academy (MLEA) where he oversaw the upgrading of the entry level, basic law enforcement curriculum to a 10-week, 500+ hour program. During this time, he also directed the establishment of the MLEA Executive Institute for chiefs and sheriffs and assisted with the restructuring of courses for supervisors and for in-service training.

Previously, Mr. Westfall served as Director of the Florida Department of Law Enforcement (FDLE) Academy responsible for training programs delivered statewide for all law enforcement agencies. His duties also included the administration of the Organized Crime Institute, the Executive Institute and the development of the Center for Advanced Law Enforcement Studies.

In prior positions, Mr. Westfall has served as Executive Assistant to the Commissioner of the Florida Department of Law Enforcement and Bureau Chief for the Division of Police Standards and Training for the State of Florida. He was charged with the enforcement of all pre-employment standards for police and corrections officers, their certification, and then decertification if they failed to maintain those norms.

Mr. Westfall began his career in law enforcement with the Alaska State Troopers where he served in a variety of functions during his four-year tenure. In 1969, he was selected as "Trooper of the Year" for the South Central Region and was recognized by the Anchorage Chamber of Commerce as "Lawman of the Year" for services provided to the Anchorage area. Prior to his entry into law enforcement, Mr. Westfall served a four-year term in the United States Marine Corps to include Vietnam.

Mr. Westfall received his BA in Criminology cum laude from Florida State University and has completed course work toward a graduate degree in Public Administration. He is also a graduate of the well well-respected FBI National Academy where he was selected as class spokesperson for the 141st Session.

Regaining Perspective: Unlikely Assistance

By Guy Rossi

It can be difficult to work in an often violent and lawless society as a law enforcement officer. Day after day, night after night, it seems like we become slaves to wherever the dispatcher sends us. There are few pats on the back and even fewer acknowledgements from the public that they appreciate what we do. We lose sight of the fact that the majority of the people we work for are law-abiding and good as they generally aren't the ones who call for services. They have families like you and I and only want to be able to move forward peacefully with their lives. I always found it ironic that my car beat was a haven for drug dealers and gangs, but on Sundays, the same streets were deserted. Even Joe drug dealer was afraid that his mama would see him on her way home from church! I got this idea one day that I would take the time to learn criminals' given names and refuse to call them by their street names when I spoke to them in front of their peers. Many so-called "Dog's" would shrink in stature a bit when called by their full birth name like Clarence, Zachary, or Matthew. At one point I began to believe that they ran from me more to avoid being embarrassed in the presence of their friends than because of the contraband they carried in their pockets. For a while, like many of you reading this, I was disheartened that I was only seeing the worst in society and became cynical that the "quiet few" were only a product of my hopeful imagination.

One spring day I began patrolling my car beat while many of my peers were still at the precinct attending a field-training officer's meeting. I was the only car in service and making the first run through the primary drug sales district. I saw a male albino who i knew had a warrant. Having never had a problem with this individual I called out my location and stepped out with him. He was literally a foot and one half shorter and at least fifty pounds lighter than I was. Standing on the sidewalk with him, I advised him that he was under arrest. I could tell that something was different about him. His eyes looked through me, and in a flash, he had put his shoulder down and got underneath me, my back slamming backwards to the curb. My portable radio dislodged from its case and slid beneath my idling patrol car. He grabbed at my sidearm and I fought furiously trying to retain my sidearm to keep from becoming a statistic. This individual, with whom I never had a problem in the past, saw me as his demon and was trying to kill me. The fight was so intense that we both ended up on the street beneath the gas tank of my car. I knew no one would be coming, as I hadn't been out long enough to concern the dispatcher. I was tired, losing the fight and was seriously thinking about shooting him off me. I tried reaching for the radio near my head but didn't dare remove the hand retaining my gun in its holster. Suddenly, the subject was pulled out from beneath the car by the legs. When I crawled out, I was amazed to see a local drunk who I had arrested several times in the past. He had kicked my assailant in the head and he now lay unconscious in the middle of the street. I quickly handcuffed him, gathered my radio, baton, and the badge that had been ripped off my uniform from the street.

I am not sure whose life this individual saved that afternoon, but to this day, I remember what he said when I asked him why he helped me. In sum and substance, he said that although he had his problems with his woman and drinking, I had always treated him with respect when he had to be arrested. He went on to say what my assailant did, "just wasn't right." It was one thing to run from the law and it was an entirely different thing to disrespect someone who had done nothing to provoke that kind of response.

Sometimes assistance comes from the most unlikely source and during the most troubling times. Although officers can never count on a Good Samaritan's help for their safety, it is a great feeling when an unlikely event can restore your faith in humanity. When you work in an area that, over time, you and your peers come to regard as a "war zone," you tend to lose sight of the fact that within the confines exist those who really want and need us there. We take an oath to protect society—it's comforting to know that sometimes it works both ways.

Guy Rossi is a retired Police Sergeant of the Rochester, New York, Police Department who specialized in patrol, recruit, field training, and defensive tactics instruction. He has been a nationally recognized law enforcement trainer since 1982. His experiences in officer survival skills have been published in over two hundred magazine articles and chapters in books on training. Upon retiring from active duty, he was employed as a Program Coordinator of Curriculum Development for the Public Safety Training Facility of Monroe Community College (MCC). Presently he is a Program Coordinator of Curriculum Development for the Homeland Security Management Institute of MCC. Guy has a Master's Degree in Adult Education—Instructional Design. He is also a proud charter member of the International Law Enforcement and Educators Training Association (ILEETA) and serves as the Editor of the prestigious ILEETA Review. In his spare time, Guy continues to peck away at law enforcement training-related articles as well as a serial killer novel he has been working on entitled, "Bloodline."

Riding For the Brand

By Roger Higby

In early 1976, I became the Chief of Police in a small city in the Central Valley of California, leaving the comfort of a larger department in the San Francisco Bay Area.

Again, I was the "new kid on the block," and I took some time to meet my peers in the neighboring communities. One of these individuals was Chief David Sundy, Sr. of the Oakdale Police Department. Oakdale is known as the "Cowboy Capital of the World." Along with Chief Henry Hessling in Waterford, we were known as the Tri-Cities agencies in Stanislaus County. We were also known as the "PA Boys," for each of us had our roots in Pennsylvania.

On my first visit to Dave's office, I saw a picture he had of a weather-beaten cowboy wearing a straw cowboy hat that was soiled and slightly torn on the brim. The face showed age lines and three days of beard growth. The caption on this picture has made a lasting impression on me for all these years. It read, "They didn't tell me everything when I hired on with this outfit." I asked Dave exactly what that caption meant and Dave gave me the biggest grin and, like the big brother that he has always been, told me that in due time, I would totally understand what that quote meant. He explained that I would learn what it meant to "ride for the brand."

I am well into the autumn of my career, and yes, I now do understand. The year was 1961; my first exposure to law enforcement was when I was hired as a police cadet at the tender age of seventeen. Naïve, gullible, starry-eyed, and impressionable, I worked the midnight shift as the desk officer, jailer, and dispatcher for a small city police department, and attended college after work. Just as the caption mentioned on the picture of the cowboy, they had not told me everything when I was hired.

I joined the army to get more training and experience by becoming a Military Policeman. Still gung-ho, I told the recruiter that I wanted to go airborne and be stationed in Germany, where my older brother had served. I even joined on the buddy plan with a friend who was in the law enforcement program at my college. In typical military fashion, I never saw jump school, my buddy and I said goodbye at Oakland Army Terminal on our first day and I was sent to Japan, not Germany.

I arrived in Japan after I completed Military Police School at Fort Gordon, Georgia and I did patrol for a total of three months. Then a sergeant found out that I could type and I became a desk clerk in the Provost Marshal's Office, which lasted about three months, and then I discovered that there was a vacancy in the Traffic Investigation Section. I did what they tell you never to do: I volunteered. It was one of the best assignments I ever had. There were only four Provost Marshal Investigators in all of Japan. We had some long days—my record for investigating collisions was fourteen in a 24-hour period. It was great training and a great experience. We worked three days on and one day off. I enjoyed this "ride," but it was time to hang up the army greens and go back to civilian police work.

Shortly after being discharged from the army, I was hired as a police officer for a mid-sized agency near San Jose. Just 22 years of age and I was sitting "high in the saddle." Like thousands of other young, progressive police officers, I went back to college to complete my associate degree in law enforcement. Although our department had no designated training officer, we were fortunate to be assigned training courses outside of our own agency. Compared to today's topics, the courses beginning in the 1960's and up to the end of the 1990's seem almost archaic by comparison to what we now study. A quick glance at some of these earlier courses gives the reader a glimpse of what drove our patrol or field operations back then. Some of these courses were:

Identi-Kit Systems	San Francisco PD
Narcotics Recognition	Cabrillo College
Nat'l Safety Council Drivers Course	Campbell PD
Alcoholic Beverage Control	Campbell PD
Chemical Agents Training	FBI @ Santa Clara PD
Law Enforcement Photography	San Jose PD
POST Supv. Academy	San Jose PD
Off. Survival Camp	San Luis Obispo
Patrol Operations Management	Cal Poly, Pomona
Internal Affairs Investigations	San Jose State University
Traffic Program Management	Cal Poly, Pomona
Homicide Investigations	DOJ, Sacramento

Compare the older style training courses to those of the 21st century (listed below):

WMD Tactical Commanders Course	Louisiana State University
WMD Advanced Tactical Operations	Louisiana State University
SEMS/NIMS/ICS Train-the-Trainer	O.E.S.—California
Active Shooter	NASA
Agro-Terrorism & Food Systems	U.C. Davis/WIFSS
Terrorism Liaison Office	San Jose P.D.
Patrol Response to Terrorism	POST/Livermore PD
Emergency Response—Terrorism	National Fire Academy

Terrorism at Beslan	San Jose State University
Counter-Terrorism	National Counter-Terrorism Academy
Management of Police Intelligence	Michigan State University
Intelligence Resources	Michigan State University

Another change over the past several decades has been the types of books that we read. One of the first must-read books that I added to my library was "No Second Place Winner" (1989), written by the legendary border patrolman, Bill Jordan. The book is still available from major bookstores. Although the book was written "back in the day," when almost all of us carried revolvers and not semi-automatic pistols, the theory of combat still remains the same. The principles of surviving a gunfight remain the same and this book remains an excellent starting point in learning street survival skills.

There are many excellent books written by contemporary authors today that should only adorn a bookshelf in your home after you have dog-eared the pages and highlighted the more important passages. Any book written by Lt. Colonel Dave Grossman (US Army—retired,) would be at the top of my list. I had been involved in more than one lethal confrontation before I had read any of his works or had the opportunity to attend one of his presentations. It was, without a doubt, money well spent. Even if you live on a very tight budget, at least buy the following three books:

1. "On Killing: The Psychological Cost of Learning to Kill in War and Society" (2009),
2. "On Combat: The Psychology and Physiology of Deadly Conflict in War and in Peace" (with Loren W. Christensen; 2008)

3. "Warrior Mindset: Mental Toughness Skills for a Nation's Peacekeepers" (with Michael J. Asken, Ph.D. and Loren W. Christensen; 2010).

For those of us who believe that more attacks will occur on American soil, I strongly suggest that you read two books published by the Archangel Group. One, entitled "Terror at Beslan: A Russian Tragedy with Lessons for America's Schools" (2005), goes into great detail on the loss of over 300 innocent lives in Beslan in 2004. More importantly, it gives the reader a road map for protecting the greatest asset we have: our children. The second book, entitled "The Green Beret in You: Living With Total Commitment to Family, Career, Sports and Life" (2007) gives the reader a *gut check* on what is important in your life as it brings to the surface those values that frame our character. The author of these two books, John Giduck, also makes presentations on the Beslan affair to both law enforcement and school authorities across the United States.

The last two books that are on the must read list are edited by Brian R. Willis and are entitled, "W.I.N.: Critical Issues in Training and Leading Warriors" (2008) and "W.I.N. 2: Insights into Training and Leading Warriors" (2009). Brian has taken a cross-section of the law enforcement community to expound on the various contemporary topics affecting every facet of law enforcement. Brian also provides personal presentations on his W.I.N. (What's Important Now) series and it is both time and money well spent to attend one of these events.

The one constant that has survived the test of time is that those of us who have taken an oath to protect and serve must never stop learning. We are constantly in motion towards improving our knowledge and skills to better serve the citizens of our communities. It is like a muscle: if it is not used, it will surely be lost.

These past five decades, I have been extremely fortunate to have a front row seat to the ever-changing world of law enforcement. I lived to see the likes of fictional characters and shows such as Dick Tracy, Joe Friday, One Adam Twelve, Police Story, Dirty Harry, RoboCop, Barney Miller, Hill Street Blues, Miami Vice, and a host of others. More importantly, I have also been fortunate to know those who were the real heroes of police work. All but a few of these hung up their badges long ago, but in the process, they passed their skills, knowledge and, yes, their baton, to a younger and more educated breed of police officer. My uncle, James Higby, lit the fire within me when I was not yet in my teens. He lived long enough to see me do an extended tour on the streets before rising through the ranks without tarnishing the badge. Through the years, I have tried to do my part to mentor and impart the skills and knowledge to the younger officers and keep that time-honored tradition alive.

All of this adventure comes with a price tag. My loved ones have become experts in providing medical care, both in the hospital and at home, while I recovered from various broken bones resulting from fights, pursuits, raids, training exercises, etc. Additionally, you will miss birthdays, weddings, anniversary's, baptisms, etc. because of manpower shortages, riot duty, dignitary protection, and a host of other requirements that preclude you from taking the day off. If you have even an ounce of integrity, you would never elect to call in sick after having a request for time off denied.

I have had the distinct pleasure of working for municipal, state, and federal agencies in my career. Each of these agencies, large or small, has been rewarding, with its own unique style of service. Ironically, of all the styles of riding that I have experienced in my career, the one that I never had an opportunity to do was to ride horses. I have driven or ridden in patrol cars and trucks, motorcycles, airplanes, boats, and helicopters, but never a horse. All in all, they were great rides and, after over six years on police motorcycles, I have that weather-beaten face to prove it. No matter which agency (or brand) I have ridden for it has been an interesting ride. I would not change it for any amount of wealth or fame.

Lieutenant Roger Higby began his full-time law enforcement career as a police cadet with Gilroy, CA. Police Department in November 1961. He was also a campus police officer with San Jose City College from 1961 to 1963 and then he joined the US Army and completed MP School at Ft. Gordon, GA.

Roger was assigned to the USARJ MP Co., Japan (later the 294th MP Co.) from January 1964 for four months before being reassigned to the 5912 CID Detachment as a Provost Marshal Traffic Investigator. He remained a traffic investigator until his discharge in June 1966. Two months later, he was employed with the Campbell Police Department and remained there for 10 years and two promotions.

In 1976, he became Chief of Police for a small city in the Central Valley of California. In 1978, he resigned from his position and became a high school teacher. In 1979, he joined the Modesto Police Department until his retirement in 1994. He worked field operations, traffic, and investigations in his 15 years with Modesto, retiring as the supervisor of the Crimes against Persons and Gang Violence Suppression units.

In 1984, while employed at Modesto PD, he joined the California Air National Guard as a Combat Arms Instructor. In June 1994, Roger was recruited by a Fortune 500 company to be a Corporate Investigator. He was ultimately promoted to the position of Corporate Director of Security before resigning when called back to active duty in the military in 2000.

In 2000, he was called back to active duty to manage a weapons conversion program. With two weeks left on that tour, the twin World Trade Center towers were attacked (September 11, 2001) and he was not released from active duty until 18 months later. He retired from the ANG in 2004 and was commissioned in the California State Military Reserve the same year. He is currently the Commandant for the Military Emergency Management Specialist Academy. He continues to serve as a consultant to special operations military personnel on weapons and tactics. He has also been fortunate to work overseas with various special groups (both military and police) in Europe, South America, and Asia.

Roger has an A.A. degree in Law Enforcement, an A.A.S. degree in Small Arms (CCAF), Bachelor's degrees in both Administration of Justice and Military Science, and a teaching credential from the State of California. Additionally, he has completed over 200 formal training courses and is court certified as an expert in both employee discipline and firearms.

He has been employed at NASA since 2003. His first assignment was as the lead trainer but after one year, he was promoted to lieutenant and returned to uniform for the third time in his career. He is currently the PM Watch Commander and an emergency management specialist.

Roger's NASA e-mail address is roger.d.higby@nasa.gov.

LT. Roger Higby
NASA's Ames Research Center Police
M/S 15-1, Moffett Field
Mt. View, CA 94035

Seek Ethical Associates and Mentors

By Todd Fletcher

There are many good points of advice for new law enforcement officers. "Always watch their hands." "Trust your instincts." "Never take your safety for granted." "Write good reports." "Plan now for your retirement." "Train like your life depends on it." These are, quite literally, words to live by and are all excellent bits of advice; but this article is going in a different direction.

During my career, I've had the honor of working for three different departments and the privilege of working beside some of the best and most talented men and women you could imagine. I've worked with officers who serve as trainers and mentors. I've worked with people who are fantastic leaders and managers, great investigators, interviewers, and bad-guy "hunters." I've worked with people who are skilled with weapons and tactics, and I've worked with people who are skilled with computers and technology. Some of these people have written wonderful articles and books sharing information about their respective areas of expertise. Many of the articles in this book are written by these same types of people. One trait each of these people has in common is that they have surrounded themselves with people who are highly ethical and moral.

Believe it or not, it is fairly easy to find people to trust with our lives. Our departments and agencies do a good job of recruiting, screening, and hiring people who are intelligent and competent. It is much more difficult to find people we can trust with our character. Throughout our careers, we will work side-by-side with people we do not necessarily like on a personal level. Yet, if any one of us is in danger, we will respond rapidly and decisively to eliminate the threat and ensure the safety of our fellow officers and our community. This does not, however, mean we should trust all of our co-workers with input on our decision-making processes or matters of our character.

Law enforcement officers do not have the luxury of making mistakes when it comes to choosing our associates. One bad choice can ruin a career. All police officers need to be careful with whom we associate ourselves, and we can do this by choosing ethical and moral people as our friends and mentors. These friends and mentors help guide career decisions and offer a trusted source of support during trying times. They can also lead us to develop our skills and talents in a way we might not have considered. Most law enforcement officers have a long memory. When an officer is perceived to have committed a personality flaw, no matter how minor, this can follow the officer around for years. Recognize this and rely on your ethical friends and mentors to guide you in correcting these perceptions.

All too often, an otherwise promising law enforcement officer's career is cut short due to ethical transgressions. As a profession, there can be no room for ethical indiscretions such as dishonesty or bad behavior. Professional law enforcement agencies and officers cannot tolerate dishonesty or deceitful behavior within our ranks. We need constant reminders of the need for principled and ethical conduct and decision making. By associating with ethical friends and mentors, we have a constant reminder of our responsibility to think and act in an ethical manner. Decisions such as whom we associate with, what we decide to do on our own time, and the types of establishments we frequent can affect our professional life and erode our credibility with the public and our co-workers. Law enforcement officers are always in the public eye, even when we are off-duty and outside our jurisdiction where we think other people will not recognize us. All of our decisions, on and off-duty, are decisions we must live with for the rest of our lives. Even when we think no one sees what we are doing, we must still live with these decisions. The problem lies in the fact that bad decisions get easier to make in the future. This is how otherwise capable officers get themselves into trouble.

We must also be able to bounce ideas off our friends and mentors without needing to worry that the information will go out to others as general knowledge. When we associate with ethical people, we are less likely to fall into this "gossip trap." Everyone claims to dislike gossip. If you take part in the gossip chain, do not be surprised when it comes back to haunt you.

It is important to be able to disagree with your friends and mentors. You must be able to disagree without the conversation leading to personal attacks. For many people, this is difficult because we allow our egos to get in the way. However, if we accept the fact that we may not have all the answers, we can come to better decisions by listening to another point of view. Your associates and mentors must be able to *call you* on your conduct or decisions, and vice versa. Do not underestimate the value of differing opinions and perspectives.

Associating with ethical people helps ensure we see more of the "big picture" instead of focusing on our own narrow view of the world. We may think we understand why someone does what they do, or we may think we understand someone else's job, but do we really know why they do what they do?

An ethical mentor can help make sure we have as much information as possible before forming an opinion about a person or a situation. We expect our communities to do this for us, yet we fail to do this for each other. For example, when someone sees a use-of-force incident, we point out the fact that they only have a small part of the overall incident. We encourage them to gather more information and to put themselves in the officer's shoes before they form an opinion or judge the officer's actions. Yet we jump to conclusions and form instant judgments of each other all the time. By relying on our ethical mentors and associates, we can ensure a better understanding of the issues at hand before jumping to unsubstantiated conclusions based on incomplete information.

Law enforcement is a noble profession. All police officers should wear their badges as symbols of honor. We are protectors of society and will always be available to serve our communities. We are skilled at arms and capable of comforting a small child in distress. We are the bedrock of a civilized society and often are held as an example of ethics, morals, and virtue. In order to maintain this standing in our communities, we need to ensure we surround ourselves with ethical people whom we trust. We are a reflection of those around us.

Sergeant Todd Fletcher is currently assigned to the Patrol Division of the Bend, Oregon Police Department. He has 15 years of law enforcement experience and is currently a defensive tactics, Taser, collapsible baton, OC, Use of Force, and Firearms Instructor. He is also an AR-15/M-4, Glock, and Smith & Wesson M&P armorer. He has written several articles regarding police training programs and has taught firearms classes to law enforcement officers nationwide. Todd has consulted and testified as an expert witness in civil and criminal cases involving police training and use of force. He can be contacted at tfletcher@ci.bend.or.us.

Social Intelligence Isn't For Sissies

By Chris Bratton

When I started my career in the early 1970's, it was all about tactics and how to stay alive and safe during the shift. That's still a priority and something we need to teach our new people on a day-to-day basis. However, what they never taught back then, and don't teach enough of today, is that there are more kinds of intelligence than just book smarts. I was lucky to have an old (even back then) sergeant who was fond of saying things like, "It's not so much what you know, but how you use it," and, "Some days, it doesn't matter what you know but rather who you know."

As one of the young Turks, I always felt like he was out of touch. I knew that it was all about having the latest and greatest equipment, training, and technical skills if I were to survive each day and go home. Little did I guess that he was right—having multiple skill sets is important, but knowing how to apply them appropriately makes the critical difference.

It took me a long time to figure out that social intelligence was a critical survival skill in this business. I always looked at social skills as touchy-feely kind of stuff that was soft and unimportant. Little did I guess that it was the stuff that makes and breaks careers and lives.

As I've gotten more experience under my belt, I realize that having a complete set of social skills can often make the difference in an encounter with the public. It can make the difference in whether a confrontation escalates into a physical altercation or de-escalates into a more "routine" citizen encounter. Perhaps one issue I had was understanding that social intelligence really is a critical skill because it deals with how to pay skilled attention to both yourself and the environment around you. It involves arranging the environment to your best advantage, positioning yourself to better protect yourself and observe your environment, posturing so that you don't antagonize others while protecting yourself, using gestures effectively, recognizing and categorizing both emotions and feelings to properly deal with them, regulating and controlling your display of emotions, displaying a professional and ready appearance, responding appropriately to the content of what is seen and heard, asking relevant questions, and making and deflecting requests. Social Intelligence training lets us look deep within and find out what we do that is distracting and annoying to others. Simple things like looking at my watch while having a conversation never seemed important to me. Little did I realize the message I was sending about how little I valued the other person in the conversation when I looked at my watch. These skills let us improve our presence and thereby create attracting behaviors that allow others to find our company pleasant and comforting. These are all things that we seem to become adept at as we move through our careers. Unfortunately, we don't approach them as a set of skills that we can teach and improve upon just like our tactical skills.

In many ways, social intelligence is a tactical skill. It is a skill set that lets us deal from a strong position, not only with citizens on the street but also internally with our co-workers and supervisors. I have seen numerous occasions where officers have reacted inappropriately to a request from a supervisor only to find themselves in serious trouble with the department. I have seen careers ended when an officer lost control of his or her emotions. I have seen marriages die for lack of paying attention to what mattered most in the relationship. I have seen officers who could escalate a scene merely by showing up and opening their mouth, and I have seen the opposite, where a situation was de-escalated and brought to a quiet conclusion through the application of social intelligence skills. Negotiators learn the verbal skill set very well during their careers and are able to end most of their incidents without harm coming to any of the participants.

I don't know why we haven't decided that our *soft* skills are as critically important as our tactical skills. For me they are one and the same. I only wish I had been fortunate enough to have someone teach me those skills early in my career. They are, in fact, the critical skills that have served me well both on the street and in the office. They are the skills that have enabled me to have a viable relationship with my children, as they have gotten older. They are the skills that let me have a relationship with a teenager. They are the skills that make my marriage a joy to be in as a partner. They are the skills that make my life richer and more enjoyable each and every day. But they are also the skills that I must constantly work to improve. Just like tactical training, social skills training requires a constant attention to detail and a constant questioning. How could I have improved the outcome of this encounter? How could I have achieved a different and better conclusion by paying closer attention? How do I repair the damage I have done to a relationship or friendship through my thoughtlessness? What does it really mean to "attend to" another person or a situation?

Social skills are much like a great car. It will run for a long time, even if we don't pay attention to it. We can drive for thousands of miles and never change the oil, check the tire pressure, rotate the tires, wash the dirt off, or clean the windows. But at some point, the car will quit—the engine will seize, the paint will flake off, and the tires will go flat. However, with a little bit of attention that great car will run on and become a classic—the envy of all of our friends and neighbors. Relationships and encounters are much the same. Without attention, they will last a while and seem to be okay. But eventually they will disintegrate unless they are attended to along the way, and attending to is what social skills are all about—learning to pay attention to ourselves, our environment, and the people that come and go each and every day.

I don't want to say that this is some kind of magic bullet. It's not. It's hard work to pay attention. But it is a skill that is just as important as knowing the proper way to make a traffic stop or search a building. It's just another skill that we have taken for granted for a long time and hoped would continue to work without improvement. It's a skill that lets us live our lives a little more fully than before. It's a skill that lets us have deeper and more fulfilling relationships both at work and at home. It's a skill that I wish I had learned years earlier in my career. Perhaps then, I would have taken better care of the people that matter the most to me as I journeyed to this point in my life and career. I might have appreciated the sergeant more, who tried to teach me how to talk to people more effectively. I might have spent more time with Bobby who taught me what it looked like to die with dignity. But at the time I didn't have the skill set that would enable me to do those things. I give thanks every day that I'm getting better at it with practice. I just wish I had known these things from the beginning.

Chris Bratton is a 37-year police veteran that is currently serving as the Chief of Police for the Elgin, Texas police department. His career spans time in patrol, investigative, and administrative divisions, and at one time or another he served as a Commander in each of those areas. His career also includes a short stint in a dual role as Police Chief and City Manager. Chris has also been fortunate to spend 30 years as a crisis negotiator. He has been instructing law enforcement officers for over 25 years in both investigative and leadership topics. Chris has provided training to officers all across the United States and Mexico. He also runs Chris Bratton Training and can be contacted either through his website at www.chrisbrattontraining.com or through the Elgin Police Department at cbratton@pd.ci.elgin.tx.us.

Start Mapping Your Career Path Now!

By Bruce A. Sokolove (a.k.a. Coach Sok)

"A wise man will make more opportunities than he finds." Those practical words of advice were uttered over four hundred years ago by the English philosopher Sir Francis Bacon. I remember hearing this during my youth but it never resonated until I was a Police Officer Candidate absorbing an interview board's question: "So, where do you see yourself in this organization in five years? In 10 years? In 20 years?" That one came right out of the blue, and I sat there trying not to act surprised while desperately trying to conjure up a response that would not sound like I was auditioning for the *supreme arrogant ass candidate of the year award*. This was a tough one and even now, over forty years later, I recall saying something about being focused on becoming a solid street cop who would leave his beat in better shape at shift's end then when I hit it out of roll call.

Wrong response! A senior Police Captain stared down and said this was very noble but they were not looking for people looking for *day jobs*. He said they were looking for career-focused individuals and then went on to say that the agency was built on the character of those who live in the present but worked toward the future one day at a time with a plan and a sense of direction. By some stroke of good fortune, I made the cut and proceeded to bust butt to figure out how to translate months of police academy curriculum and apply it to the streets long before the days when formal Field Training and Evaluation Programs and Field Training Officers would expedite that transfer. Literally surviving the Probationary Year was goal number one and, unbelievably, it flew by. Two years later, I found myself on a power shift with a dynamic command and supervisory crew that created a tight work group, functioning more like family than a shift. I was about to encounter my supreme mentor in the form of the street boss, a Staff Sergeant 10 years my senior.

Readers, this would be a really good time to bookmark this page and reach back to volume one of "If I Knew Then: Life Lessons From Cops on the Street" (2010), turn to page 83 and read Calgary Police Services Inspector Cliff O'Brien's outstanding piece on "How to Find a Good Mentor." Take heed of those laying in wait for the new guys and the fresh meat that do not know any better. I encountered more than a few of these *hidden-agenda masters* along the way, but I was blessed because my Patrol Shift Staff Sergeant was there to serve more like a shift coach than just a street boss and assessor of street performance. Best of all, he was a totally transparent mentor-in-residence. No hidden agenda guy here. He was the embodiment of the axiom that "if you take care of your people, they will take care of the mission." Sarge knew how to create exceptionally motivated and self-reliant street cops. This was sheer luck of the shift bid on my part. The Sarge was about to become the most impacting person in a still fresh career and would quietly assist me with shifting into career overdrive.

Sarge's first kernel of wisdom was to resist letting time and the occasional pop-up opportunities of position postings dictate my career path. Looking back, this was pretty much like the Robin Williams character John Keating, the English teacher, in the movie "Dead Poets Society,"[1] exhorting. *Carpe Diem* to his high school students (albeit twenty years earlier). Sarge literally told me to take control of my career

---

1. Dead Poets Society, DVD, directed by Peter Weir (USA: Touchstone Pictures, Silver Screen Partners IV, 1989).

assignment options and never float with the tide of duty days hoping to end up on the right career path. That advice morphed into a practical guided tour on taking personal responsibility for career development. He said that this would not occur unless I took immediate responsibility to mentally create a mind map and rehearse a number of different career scenarios. The first step was to acknowledge consciously that accountability started with me if I truly wanted a meaningful career where I would contribute and make a difference. Sarge always reminded me that when you control your thoughts, you control your future, and that I would never see it unless I truly believed it. This was an introduction to visualization and imagery long before I had a clue how powerful and real world those concepts are. Sidebar: never judge a book by its cover. The Sarge was an Agricultural Science baccalaureate and an escapee from a centennial farm family, not a psychology major. I was soon to discover that he also had a PhD.

A few weeks before my first semiannual performance evaluation with this team, the Sarge provided a heads up by telling me that we would be formally discussing the last six months of street activity and we would then shift towards focusing on proactively taking control of the next six months. This was a new experience. I was directed to start preparing with the admonition that I would never achieve my dreams if they did not become goals. For emphasis, he told me that I would never arrive at a career destination without a clear picture of where I was going, and then provided a word equation: *Goals + Action = Success*. Practically and timely, he pulled down Webster's dictionary from his shelf and showed me that *success* precedes *work* only between the bound covers. He immediately got, and held my attention with that one.

Sarge also underscored the fact that I would never achieve my career aspirations without mastering the day-to-day inner drive to become a proactive street cop. There were no in-car computers back in the day (or for many years to follow), but he aptly described the uniforms that cleared roll call and simply drove their marked unit through the streets like a mechanical scarecrow attempting to randomly scare away crime and disorder. He added that these were the reactive guys who waited for Dispatch to tell them what to do and where to go. They were also the cops who would tag an occasional traffic stop to make numbers. Sarge intoned that the real cops not only caught their runs but also knew proactively what to *do* with the unassigned time when there were no calls waiting in queue, or the need to back up other units, and that traffic enforcement was only a part of the equation.

Fortunately, my assigned patrol beat was a virtual Disney Land of activity and opportunities with no shortage of street folks, walk-aways from the lunatic fringe, bad guys, and lots of crimes against persons and property. You only had to throw in the vehicular and pedestrian issues to make it a virtual all-you-want-to-graze buffet table of what's-happening-now activity, so it was no stretch of the imagination to see what the mission could look like.

It was time to hit the books and cram on goal setting. This was no short task. Most of the literature in the pre-Internet age was located in business administration textbooks, but everything I read reinforced what Sarge had said. Principle #1: you cannot expect total success without constructing an action plan and blueprint. Another stroke of good fortune fell into my lap when one of the senior team members accurately read my vacant stare when I exited the street boss's office. He promptly pulled me aside to share his goal setting experience the first time he was on Sarge's opening day line-up card. He spared me untold hours of anxiety wondering where to start by telling me just to *get SMART*. He proceeded to tell me that Sarge expected the goals to meet the *SMART* criteria where each would be the following:

- S = Specific,
- M = Measurable,
- A = Attainable,
- R = Realistic,
- T = Timely.

Principle #2: Time to embrace another one of Sarge's truisms: *never suffer from constipation of creativity*. Fortunately, I knew my limitations, and recognized that I was a very visual learner and would have to literally *see* activity targets as something more than verbal entries on the roll call logs or pin maps on the squad room walls. Little did I know that Sarge was setting the stage for Problem-Oriented Policing more than a decade before this would become the policing concept du jour.

Necessity became the mother of invention for the moment. Fortuitously, we had access to what was affectionately called the *Xerox machine* (say good-bye carbon paper) that included this amazing feature where you could actually reduce the size of the printed page. In went over-sized beat maps and out came 8.5" x 11" pages of the same beats that now fit snugly into three-hole punched notebook plastic sheet protectors. The final piece of the puzzle was to figure out how to use various colors of non-permanent marking pens to highlight the activity targets that would serve as my six-month street crime/activity suppression goals— something like a coach's grease board back in the day before clean erase magic markers.

Batter up. Before I knew it, I was sitting in Sarge's office for my performance review and showing him my proposed six-month goals (written on 3" x 5" index cards,) along with the physical target areas duly noted in a swash of color-coded and indexed map entries. Sarge provided some tweaking and suggestions along with an atta boy for recognizing that you can't hit a target if you cannot see it, and you cannot see a target that you do not have. I was batting .1000 so far and figured that I made the first cut on the six-month goal setting detail.

Principle #3: It would take years to comprehend fully that Sarge understood how critical it was to share goals and the action plan with a *trusted other* who would be supportive and who would always be available to provide no-nonsense, timely feedback. Sarge made time for the periodic face-to-face discussions to assess progress, or simply assist me with adjusting the action plan when results were not happening.

Sarge's final words of advice brought me full circle to Sir Francis Bacon's wise words by reinforcing that I had a firm grasp of how to stay task-focused with short-term goal setting, but that was only a small part of the puzzle. He told me to swap lenses to see the wide-angle view of my nascent career and figure out how to create the opportunities to execute a viable career path, not just think in half-year chunks.

Principle #4: Sarge's best advice was to not just *look* at what others were doing, but rather *study* how they were getting it done and start to identify those specialty mentors who might be willing to share their expertise. I started looking at Evidence Technicians, Investigators, Crime Analysts, Trainers, and Assistant Prosecuting Attorneys (among others,) in a completely different light. This made all the difference whenever I would encounter an obstacle or needed a fresh set of eyes to find options. You will be amazed how many mentors will show up in your career and that will make all the difference.

It doesn't hurt to be a bit of a futurist along the journey without resorting to psychic readings from the local Fortune Tellers. One of my cohorts on shift kept talking about the impact that computers would have beyond vehicle registration and wants/warrants data retrieval. He promptly headed off to the local community college to consume every course in the then, short catalog of offerings. A real world example of seeing and preparing for the future. This cop literally created a much needed job position, wrote the position description, and was the right person at the right time to staff it. Think about what you need to do to make yourself the best person in the right place at the right time. That will not occur with blind luck or by accident. Start setting SMART goals to create your personal Career Vision Statement. These will be the essential components of your career action plan.

Keep in mind that this is a long journey with a zillion small steps. Never fear falling short. Embrace the errors and learn from them. Above all, never allow the fear of failure to create the psychological equivalent of self-benching. That is a guaranteed derailment plan that will prevent you from actualizing your Career Vision Statement.

And never forget the old English proverb that *what goes around, comes around*. Never permit yourself to become a taker. The real deal cops always give back and share their mastery with those that have a genuine spirit of inquiry and work ethic to take their career to the next level. It gets easier to figure out and separate the contenders from the pretenders. It's a great feeling of satisfaction when you can honestly say that you've left your House in better shape than when you found it and not be a legend in your own mind after uttering it. Enjoy the journey.

Carpe diem.

Bruce Sokolove, aka, Coach Sok, is a dye-in-the-wool green and white Michigan State University Spartan (last graduate school class of the School of Police Administration and Public Safety,) who survived a career of policing in the People's Republic of Ann Arbor, Michigan, home to that other University. Coach Sok commenced his law enforcement career with the North Adams, Massachusetts Police Department while finishing his undergraduate studies at the Massachusetts College of Liberal Arts. He has also served at the Ann Arbor Police Department as Undersheriff of the Washtenaw County Sheriff's Department and with the United State Marine Corps.

Coach Sok is the President of "Field Training Associates," providing law enforcement training and consulting assistance for generations of Field Training Officers and Street Bosses across North America. Coach spends a fair amount of time in the courts assisting agencies in defending against allegations of wrongful discharge and negligent training. He has provided workshop presentations at the International Association of Chiefs of Police and at the FBI National Academy at Quantico, Virginia—the Crossroads of the United States Marine Corps. Coach's articles have appeared in Law and Order, and Police Chief Magazine over the years. Coach Sok can be reached at fieldtraining@mac.com.

Take All Training Seriously. Live the Tactical Lifestyle!

By Steven Mosley

Over the years, I have had the opportunity to serve with some of the greatest law enforcement officers and professionals in the world. It has been 27 years since I started my law enforcement career and I have had some amazing training experiences that truly helped shape my life. My path has been fairly straightforward: Military Police, Corrections Officer, Police Officer, Deputy Sheriff, and then Federal Special Agent. I continue to grow each and every day, absorbing what is useful and putting it into practice; however, if there is one thing I wish I would have known when I started two decades ago, it is the philosophy of taking all training seriously.

Unfortunately, I have sat in many a class, spaced-out, and saying to myself, "I will never need or use this stuff. This instructor is terrible. Where did they get this person? I cannot believe I wasted my day off to come to this training." Every one of us has possibly had one of these thoughts. Nevertheless, I am going to suggest to you that once you have had this kind of thought, it will be but a few short minutes, perhaps days, or maybe even years later when you find yourself in the middle of a situation and say to yourself, "Damn. I wish I had paid more attention in that class." Trust me when I say that you must take all training seriously. You truly never know when some little bit of wisdom or information may come in handy for future use.

Brian Willis is always talking about WIN—"What's Important Now." This is so powerful. Words to live by, for sure. Think about WIN the next time you are sitting in a training class and remember that the most important thing you can do is absorb all the information the instructor is providing. Figure out a way to make it stick inside that brain of yours! Even if you walk away with one to three new concepts or ideas, you have used the time wisely. Perhaps the next call you are on will test you as you have never been tested before. If you paid attention and gave prior consideration to how to apply your newly acquired knowledge, you could very well save your life or your partner's life in this critical situation.

Let us take CPR training as an example. Some people find it boring and zone out for long stretches of time. Shake to establish consciousness. Ask if they are okay. Have someone dial 911 for assistance. Check the airway for obstructions. Check the pulse, and give breaths and compressions. Without learning or practicing these simple tasks in earnest, some may easily forget and omit them during a crisis. Do you really want to be trying to figure out what to do next while you are in the middle of saving someone's life? I think not!

It has been my experience that life has a way of slapping you in the face when you least expect it. You need to have a plan of attack to deal with the unexpected because solid mental preparation will help propel you forward. Taking your training seriously will certainly aid you in building a better mindset. Here are some ideas for getting the most out of your next training opportunity (all training provides an opportunity for growth!):

>   Take notes,
>   Ask questions,

Get involved in the class and be mentally present, Be an active participant and student.

All of these will go a long way toward retention. I also suggest that upon completing your training, review, review, and review some more. Reviewing your notes helps tremendously with retention—rewrite them while they are still fresh in the mind. You should probably do this for several weeks following the training. One other trick for retention is to immediately teach the skills you learned to someone else. At a minimum, discuss what you learned with someone else.

Aside from training, if there is one piece of advice that I could give my fellow officers, it is this: Follow and live the "The Tactical Lifestyle." The concept of Tactical Lifestyle is borrowed from my good friend and excellent trainer, Dennis Martin. If you do not know Dennis, please visit his website at www.cqbservices.com. He is one of the best among trainers. The Tactical Lifestyle focuses on a blend of Mindset, Tactics, Skills, and Kit acquired during training and used every day in travel, work, home, and leisure activities.

Proper mindset is truly a critical component of the Tactical Lifestyle that I cannot stress enough. It is often stated by some of the great gunfighters that combat is 90 percent mental, 5 percent skill, and 5 percent luck. Mindset, as it applies to the Tactical Lifestyle, requires the understanding of two key concepts: Colonel Boyd's OODA Loop and Threat Evaluation. In my opinion, you need to start your research and study of Boyd's decision loop and its four phases immediately: Observation, Orientation, Decision, and Action. As a warrior, understanding and applying this concept can be life saving. Unfortunately, it has been overlooked by many. Do not be one of the many. As far as threat evaluation is concerned, imagine realistic threats that you could face any day, and have a plan to deal with each of them. Also, imagine a positive outcome for each threat— this is crucial. When time is available, role-play the scenarios with fellow officers, and find a viable solution to each threat.

Tactics is the next part of the Tactical Lifestyle. You should develop a set of core tactics to deal with a variety of situations. Your tactics should become habitual. Obviously, the only way to do that is through constant, serious practice. I call this practicing with intent. Too often, we just go through the motions during training. Do not fall into this trap. When you are training, TRAIN! You can play later—I am all for that aspect of life, also. You should also practice integrated team tactics. We must often work with other individuals on special tasks, so it would be extremely beneficial if our tactical thinking matched.

Understand that in living the Tactical Lifestyle, you must practice skills that work. This is just a short list of skills that you should be honing:

> Defensive tactics,
> Firearms,
> Immediate weapon use,
> First aid,
> Driving skills.

The list could and should be endless. The main point is to practice effective skills that transfer effectively from the gym to the street. Remember, stress is the prime consideration when talking about skills. The skills that you are practicing must work under extreme duress. If they do not work in the controlled environment of the training hall, then they will most certainly not work on the street.

Lastly, you must know your Kit; i.e., your equipment. Please make sure your kit is serviced and in working condition. Do not carry kit that you do not know how to use! It is great to have the latest and greatest equipment, but wouldn't it benefit us more if we actually knew how to utilize it during a crisis? I believe strongly in keeping it simple, and it should be ready and available when needed.

Well, there you have it; my two cents worth of information based on my experiences. The law enforcement profession is a very noble occupation, though you will not receive many pats on the back, raises, or awards. At the bad end of the spectrum, you may very well expect to be assaulted, spat on, possibly shot at, and all other sorts of nasty things during the course of your career. You have chosen this profession for your own reasons. I only ask you to consider seriously two things: First, take your training seriously, because you just never know when you will need the information you are being taught; second, live the Tactical Lifestyle. Proper mindset, solid and proven tactics, the development of practical hard and soft skills, and the knowledge of your equipment will not only go a very long way to ensure your survival, but will give you the edge to WIN! Thank you and best wishes.

Steven Mosley is currently a Supervisory Special Agent with the Department of Homeland Security. He has been a certified Police Defensive Tactics and Firearms Instructor for over 20 years. He is also a Senior Instructor under the British Combat Association and is an Instructor in the Filipino Martial Arts under Guro Dan Inosanto. For more information on Steven, check out his website at www.combathard.com. He can be contacted at stevenmosley@hotmail.com.

The Four Ranges of a Fight

By Kelly Keith

There are so many things that I can think of that I wish I knew when I first hit the streets of Winnipeg in 1988. Now that I instruct law enforcement cadets in Atlantic Canada, I realize how hard it is to put everyone's ideas of what is important into one program that is *not* 5 years long. Seeing that the main topic I teach is Control Tactics, I will stick with the topic.

The majority of control tactics time is spent going through the actual techniques in the gym. However, just as important as these techniques is the need to understand the different ranges of a fight, how a WWII Military tactic is just as applicable to policing as the winning pilot fights, and being able to read the body language/pre-assaultive cues of a suspect rather than finding out you are in an altercation when the subject first hits you.

The Four Ranges of a Fight

In my personal martial arts training I realized very quickly that if you want to win against various fighters you need at the very least to be competent and have a good understanding of the four ranges that may come into play in any fight. If I come across a boxer, I need to understand and be able to deal with striking range, etc. Even though I have personally practiced each range I had not really made the connection to teaching *each range with each weapon* in police work until I went to a lecture by my friend, Sergeant Jeff Quail, who is a Winnipeg Police Officer. I now teach every cadet how to use every weapon applicable in each range. The four ranges are posturing, striking, close quarters, and ground.

Posturing: This is the range where the suspect and the officer are outside of each other's personal weapon (arms/legs) striking distance. The suspect may have his fists clenched and be telling the officer he is going to kick his ass but, at the range that he is saying this, he is not capable of hitting you. As Law Enforcement Officers, we do not have to wait to get hit before we defend ourselves and ensuring that you have the proper weapon at the ready in this range is crucial!

Striking: This is the distance where the suspect's or the officer's weapons are within striking distance. At this distance, a jab, cross, front kick, baton swing, etc., can connect. Remember that *action* is faster than *re-action*. Thus, all things being equal, if you are standing within a suspect's striking range he/she can hit you—at least the first time—every time. This is why we always stand outside of the suspect's striking range in the reactionary gap. When a suspect does get within this range, we need to be comfortable in how to best deal with it. We may decide that it is best to change distances both by disengaging to posturing range and changing weapons, or if you are superior in strength and tactics, you may change distances by taking the suspect to the ground and handcuffing.

Close quarters: This is commonly known as the clinch position. This position is where knees, elbows, foot stomps, head butts, etc., can connect. The same principles as above apply for this distance.

Ground: No matter how we end up on the ground, there are very different dynamics to a ground fight than a stand-up fight. There are times when we would want to take the suspect to the ground to get him/her in handcuffs. Then there are other times, such as when the suspect is on top of you, that you need to understand the limitations of being on the ground and how to get to your feet. With mixed martial arts becoming more and more mainstream, it is imperative that you understand this range and how to get the suspect into handcuff position or how to fight to your feet.

If the officer can read pre-assaultive cues correctly, understand how to create distance, use a barrier, and draw the appropriate weapon, the officer can then dictate the ranges of the confrontation on most occasions. The key is to know what to do in each fighting range with each tool and, if it is advantageous for you to change range, you need to know how.

OODA Loop

Colonel John Boyd of the U.S. Air Service (retired) first came up with the OODA loop in WWII. Today, it still has great relevance in both the military and law enforcement. In this article, I will not go into the history behind it; however, I strongly urge you to do some research on it!

The OODA loop stands for:

Observe: The safety-conscious officer will observe their surroundings, understand where the doors are and whether they open in or out, look at a chesterfield in a domestic situation as a barrier rather than a chesterfield, and look for any potential weapons in the room (baseball bat, hockey stick, etc.). A safety-conscious officer will always attempt to observe the suspect before the suspect observes the officer and observe anything in the suspect's hands.

Orient: This stage is critical to your safety! It refers to how fast the officer can analyze the suspect's actions and put them into context. The faster we can put the suspect's actions into context, the faster we can react. The key then is to turn the tables and have the suspect re-acting to our actions! If a suspect with the intent to shoot us has drawn his or her gun on us before we have the chance to draw, it is too late to try to outdraw him. We must make the suspect orient himself to us through movement and utilize this time to draw our gun and return fire. The more you practice spinal tuning ("what if/when then thinking,") at calls, the more you participate in reality based training, the more experience you gain with whatever actions the suspect is doing and determine how skilled you are in the force required to control the situation, the better you will be at dealing with this stage.

Decide: Now that the officer has oriented his/herself to the situation, the next step is the decision to act and how fast the officer can make this decision. This decision can be to arrest and handcuff or to use deadly force, depending on the circumstances. Key factors at this stage are your knowledge of the law and your grounds to re-act with the proper amount of force.

Act: We spend most of our time in training dealing with the "act" portion of the OODA loop. The "act" is the physical action required to complete the sequence such as the pulling of a trigger or the arm going forward for a strike. The time it takes you to act on the situation can also be influenced by your knowledge of the positions of your weapons on your duty belt, draw times, and your ability to acquire the target with whatever weapon you are using.

Understanding and beating the suspect using the OODA loop is a key ingredient to winning our confrontations and is well worth studying, understanding, and putting it into practice.

Pre-Assaultive Cues

A subject may give clues as to his or her intentions. An obvious attack sign would be verbal threats and/or verbal abuse. The better we are at reading peoples' physical signs of attack *before* they attack us, the better defense—the better we can verbally address their intentions before they follow through with a threat, and the better prepared we will be if they attack us! If we see a suspect showing pre-assaultive cues, in most cases distance is our friend. Understanding how barriers and cover will assist you and then being very capable in your communication skills to de-escalate the situation can have you either avoiding the situation or, if unavoidable, winning it! The following is a list of pre-assaultive cues:

- Ignoring the officer;
- Repetitious questioning;
- Aggressive verbalization—yelling, swearing;
- Emotional venting;
- Refusing to comply with a lawful request;
- Hiding;
- Ceasing all movement;
- Invasion of personal space;
- Adopting an aggressive stance—blade body, lower center of gravity, shifting weight;
- Changing posture—stands taller, sets head and shoulders, moves away or moves closer, points, forms fist and/or loads the arm;
- Face becomes red, lips separate to show teeth, breathing becomes faster, perspiration appears on the skin, lips become tight as breathing (though

still rapid,) deepens, the face then loses its flush to become pale;
- Looks away or stares through people (1000-yard stare);
- Aggression is redirected to something/someone else, such as breaking pencils, kicking, chairs, yelling at bystanders;
- The individual may bob or rock while shifting eyes to possible targets—head will come down, chin tucked, eyebrows tightened and dropped;
- Rolling-up sleeves or taking-off shirt;
- Scanning the area;
- Exaggerated body movements to relieve stress;
- Stretching in preparation.

In policing, one key ingredient in getting you home at the end of each shift is knowledge. Gaining this knowledge from officers who have "been there and done that" is invaluable!

Kelly Keith is a 23-year veteran of policing. He is an inspector with the Atlantic Police Academy and instructs physical fitness, officer safety, use of force, and firearms. He spent 13 years with the Winnipeg Police, 4 years with the Victoria Police, and is now in his sixth year at the Atlantic Police Academy. He has worked general patrol, vice division, plain-clothes detective work, and community-based policing.
He is an instructor in a number of use of force and firearms disciplines and has testified in court on many occasions as a use of force expert.

Kelly is a second-degree black belt in Jiu-Jitsu—(bronze medalist at the World Jiu-Jitsu Championship) and has studied many other disciplines. He is also a certified personal trainer, certified strength and conditioning instructor, and a certified sports nutrition specialist.

The Power of Questions

By Brian Willis

"You must constantly ask yourself these questions: Who am I around? What are they doing to me? What have they got me reading? What have they got me saying? Where do they have me going? What do they have me thinking? And most important, what do they have me becoming? Then ask yourself the big question: Is that okay? Your life does not get better by chance, it gets better by change." Jim Rohn

For most of my 25 year police career and my 20 plus years as a law enforcement trainer I have thought that the ability to make change and influence behavior came from always having answers to questions and solutions to problems. I mistakenly thought that my job as a law enforcement professional and trainer was to be a problem solver and I assumed that meant I had to always come up with the right answers and solutions.

Over the past 30 years I have discovered that the real ability to create lasting change comes in the form of questions. Questions, especially open-ended ones, help to uncover information, wisdom, knowledge, hopes, dreams, motives, choices, answers, and most importantly more questions. This applies to your personal and professional life. Let me share some examples.

Asking more questions of victims would have helped me gain more information about both the victim as a person and the crime. Those questions would have helped those victims feel like someone truly cared about them as a person as opposed to just being another statistic. Asking more questions of suspects would have drawn out more detailed and varied information, unveiled more offences, and provided me with an insight into how criminals think. All of this would have made me a better investigator and resulted in more solved crimes. Too often we just ask the basic questions to fill in the appropriate boxes on the report and then move on to the next call.

Asking more questions of my children would have given me a greater insight into what was going on in their lives and about their fears, hopes, and dreams. I would have learned more about their friends and experiences at school. I am not talking about interrogating children and treating them like suspects. I am talking about creating a habit of engaging in discussions where you ask open-ended questions and truly listen to the answers. All this would have helped me be a better father.

Asking more questions of the people I was given the privilege of supervising and leading would have provided me with an even deeper understanding of what was important to them on both a personal and professional level. Those questions would have helped to develop me into a better leader.

Asking more questions of my wife (we are approaching our 30th anniversary) would have helped me understand what it was like to be the wife of a cop. It would have given her a greater chance of being heard, of being understood and of feeling more valued in the relationship. As a result, I would have been a better husband.

For some time as a patrol supervisor, incident commander and trainer I mistakenly thought the key to debriefings was to Tell More and Ask Less. Tell officers what they did right, what they did wrong and what they need to do differently. I was under the mistaken belief that this methodology would change behavior and improve performance. Occasionally it did, but rarely to the extent that I hoped for. It has taken me 20 years but I believe I have discovered that the key to effective debriefings is to Ask More—Tell Less. As Dan James says *"Asking questions will get you the performance you are after far better than dictating demands."* Questions help everyone involved to learn and grow through self-reflection which is a more powerful tool for creating lasting change than being told what to do by someone else. Questions such as:

> How did you feel about your performance?
> What did you do well?
> What did you learn from the experience?
> What would you like to do differently in a similar situation in the future?
> What do you need from me for you to be more successful in the future?

One specific question I wish I had known very early in my life is the question that I now refer to as Life's Most Powerful Question—What's Important Now? This one question would have helped me in a number of ways:

- It would have slowed me down when I was racing to a call that in no way justified the risk to myself, my partner and the members of the public who were on the roadway.
- It would have gotten me off my ass on those days where I used being tired as an excuse not to work out.
- It would have helped me eat healthier.

- It would have made me wear my body armor on those days when I was to lazy or too stupid not to wear it.
- It would have made me take a step back and reconsider before rushing through that door to make the arrest that could have waited until we had better intelligence or more resources.
- It would have helped me set aside my ego and terminate some pursuits.
- It would have gotten me to spend more time both at the range and dry firing to improve my firearms skills.
- It would have inspired me to attend more conferences and courses at my own expense early in my career.
- It would have motivated me to read more in the early parts of my life and my career.
- It would have made me realize the benefits of maximizing the funding available through the city to help pay for secondary education earlier in my career.
- It would have inspired me to spend less time at work and more time at home especially in the last 8 ½ years of my career when as a Training Sergeant I put in close to 7000 hours of unpaid overtime.
- It would have driven me to seek out training and skills outside of law enforcement to make me a better presenter and trainer.

One question I wish I had never learned as a cop is "Do you want to do this the easy way, or the hard way?" It seems that the hard way always involved a fight which usually resulted in someone being injured and was too often followed by a citizen's complaint. As Peter Drucker says *"The most serious mistakes are not being made as a result of wrong answers. The truly dangerous thing is asking the wrong question."*

I would encourage you to do three things in both your personal and professional life:

> Take the time to ask more questions.
> Take the time to actively listen to those answers.
> Repeat.

Brian Willis is an internationally recognized leader, speaker and trainer. He draws upon his 25 years of law enforcement experience as a member of the Calgary Police Service and his 20 plus years of training experience to provide cutting edge training to law enforcement officers and trainers throughout North America. Brian operates the innovative training company Winning Mind Training and is the editor of the highly acclaimed books: W.I.N.: Critical Issues in Training and Leading Warriors; W.I.N. 2 Insights Into Training and Leading Warriors; and If I Knew Then: Life Lessons From Cops on the Street (www.warriorspiritbooks.com). Brian serves as the Deputy Executive Director for ILEETA and is a member of NTOA, ITOA, IALEFI, and the Canadian Association of Professional Speakers. Brian can be reached through his website at www.winningmindtraining.com.

The Struggle Within

By Harvey Hedden

It is an unfortunate fact that stress kills more law enforcement officers than gunfire. An important source of stress is not frustration with the courts, the public we serve, or criminals, but the organization where we work. Many officers complain that there is little justice within their criminal justice agency. They become frustrated but are unable or unwilling to change this condition, or even to talk openly about it with their peers and supervisors. Unresolved and unexpressed, this frustration can lead to problems in their performance, their relationships, and their health in general. To counter this threat, new officers need to better understand the workplace and have tools to help them influence their relationship with the organization.

In many organizations, the informal political structure is far more important than the official structure and chain of command. In assessing the agency, we can look at management to determine the qualifications for success. In too many cases, hard work and proficiency are not rewarded but are a source of potential criticism. The more cases an officer handles, the greater the possibility that someone will complain about some aspect of that work. I recall a seasoned detective's motto, "Big cases, big problems; little cases, little problems; and no cases, no problems." If you write a lot of tickets, not only do those who receive them complain but so might the court officer or the other officers on your shift because they are concerned you will make them look unproductive. I can recall promotional evaluations in which managers said they could not recall hearing anything bad about a candidate. Unfortunately, that was because the candidate did little work and showed even less initiative. In some organizations, accolades and promotions go to those who can get along with supervision and management and don't make any problems for them. Those who are unable to get along may look at the agency as a real adversary. A mistrust of management can spread to supervision, peers, and even our family.

If you are lucky enough to recognize this in an agency that you are thinking about working for, or that you recently joined and you have prospects for alternative employment, you might well consider a change in agencies. Lacking that option there are still methods to help officers manage their relationship with the agency and maintain a positive attitude towards work. Just like survival on the street, two of the most important resources the officer can possess for survival within the organization are a disciplined mind and interpersonal communication skills.

We must first define for ourselves what it is to be a professional law enforcement officer. Next, we need to determine the agency's definition and determine where we have common ground. If you are not true to your own beliefs and values, and try to conform to those you do not believe in, you will experience stress. Fortunately, your definition and the official definition of the agency may not be all that different. The challenge is to cause evaluation of your performance to be judged by the formal rather than the informal norms of the agency. We can accomplish this through effective communication with our peers, field-training officers, and supervisors, regarding the agency's core values and performance standards.

New police officers are often so eager to show that they are ready to handle anything that they avoid asking for advice and input. Consequently, they are viewed as overconfident and naïve. It is not a sign of weakness to ask about what is expected of us or what we can do to perform better, but rather an indication that we value the input of others with more experience. The mark of a true professional in any field is that they are always striving for self-improvement. Learning does not end at the academy and should be a lifelong process or we will stagnate. Even if you do not agree with their opinion, you can at least understand how you might be evaluated by others. Avoid debating with senior officers and supervisors as it makes it less likely you will receive their honest input in the future.

You are destined to make mistakes on the job. The traditional response in law enforcement has been "cover your butt (or another term for that body part)." There was a time when much of what an officer did went unobserved and unreported and this was not difficult to accomplish. But every new generation of law enforcement is under greater scrutiny and observation. Covering up is not just impractical and dishonest; it is unprofessional because we do not attempt to correct the error. An officer found to have covered up a small error may be imagined to have successfully covered up much larger ones. Performance problems or errors should be looked at as opportunities for improvement and we should keep our own record of them. Once, when a supervisor had summoned me for a chewing out, I took responsibility for the error, told him why I had made it, and provided a plan to make it unlikely it would happen again to me or another officer. I then asked if he could offer any improvements on the plan before I reduced it to writing and sent it to him. This removed the adversarial nature of the meeting and made the supervisor's job easier.

Keeping your own personal file has advantages to you and those who would evaluate your work. In addition to keeping track of areas in which you are improving performance, it seems that when you perform your job really well, there is no one around to notice. Use your personal file to keep track of calls and problems that you handled particularly well. Although valuable for personal evaluation, don't wait for the annual review to discuss your performance but make it an ongoing process. This is particularly true if your supervisor is unhappy with you. Don't let that issue fester and grow, deal with it while the event is still fresh.

If you have had one of those unnoticed successes, you should try to find a way to get that information to your supervisor. Most of us have an aversion to those who brag about themselves. There is a subtle art to promoting yourself, (I would rather describe it as providing helpful evaluative information,) without appearing to be bragging. You must be able to engage your intended receiver in small talk. Most people like to talk about themselves. You must then look for an opportunity to provide the information concisely as it relates to the conversation more as a related story than self-promotion. If asked, you can then provide more details. If applicable, you should also credit anyone that helped you with the issue. If, because of this event, you learned something new, or if you utilized training that you received to reach that success, you might use this as your introduction of the subject and reduce the "I" messages in your communication. Don't forget to promote the good works of others and, on occasion, you might be surprised that they will return the favor.

There is nothing wrong with wanting to be a line officer and avoiding promotion. This is the job in the agency that all the other positions are designed to support. Become a master of your job but always be hungry for more knowledge. If you desire promotion, work hard for that as well. Learn all you can about that position, talk to people who are a success in that rank, study test material, take practice tests and practice oral interviews to give you the best opportunity to achieve your goal.

Learning to navigate through the informal structure and rules of the agency can be frustrating. No text or formal instruction can assure success. What works for others may not work for you. It is important to have resources outside of law enforcement such as a spouse, relative, or close friend to whom you can express both your successes and frustrations, and from whom you can receive support and affirmation. If you hide these things from those you care for and try to cope alone, you may eventually drive them away from you. Some day you will leave this job and it is most important that you and those you care for are not damaged or destroyed as a result of your employment.

You are a unique individual and you will be so as an officer. Don't play their game, pretending to be something you are not. You must know who you are and in what you believe. If your sense of worth is solely tied to the opinions of others, you will be confused and frustrated. As Johann Wolfgang von Goethe said, "How can you come to know yourself? Never by thinking, always by doing. Try to do your duty, and you'll know right away what you amount to."

Harvey Hedden is a nationally known law enforcement trainer with 33 years of law enforcement experience and 29 years as a trainer. He served for most of his career with the Kenosha County, WI Sheriff's Department, attaining the rank of Lieutenant. Harvey commanded drug enforcement task forces for more than two decades, and also supervised his department's Hostage Negotiation Unit, Marine Unit, and Dive Team. He is currently the Chief of the Paddock Lake, WI Police. Harvey served as the Deputy Executive Director of the International Law Enforcement Educators and Trainers Association until he accepted the position of Executive Director in 2009.

The Warrior's Path

By Charles "Chip" Huth

I began my career in law enforcement in 1991. The culmination of my academy training was the realization of a life-long dream. I was incredibly enthusiastic and could not wait to pin the badge on and fight crime. I worked even harder after academy graduation to further prepare physically and develop great skill with the weapons I needed to police my community. I jumped in with both feet, as it were, and never looked back. I sought to fashion myself after the warriors who had come before me. In my mind, I was justice personified, and I was prepared to stand tall to defend the innocent sheep from the ravenous wolves that preyed upon them. Good and bad, black and white, it was just as I pictured it and I had a front row seat for the wildest show I could ever imagine.

While my enthusiasm has not waned much, I have had many things put into perspective over the course of the past twenty years. Chief among these revelations is the fact that the citizens we serve are not objects—or sheep—to be dealt with as quickly and efficiently as possible. While they come in all shapes, sizes, and flavors, weak, strong, and everything in between, the people we are sworn to defend are truly human beings with needs, hopes, dreams, and fears similar to my own. At first glance, a passive observer might consider that fact to seem like an obvious observation. However, as a young officer, I was taught early on that the only way to be safe and effective on the street was to construct categories for people and ensure that the community members I dealt with in various contexts fit nicely into one of those categories. My vernacular expanded to include phases like, "this jungle," and "these animals." These coping mechanisms brought some sense of clarity to what was otherwise a very ambiguous job. It was an efficient way of doing business, but it fell far short of any substantial degree of effectiveness.

As I progressed in my career, my maturity allowed me to become self-critical. I was no longer operating from a position of insecurity and was free to consider alternative viewpoints. I began to look at the duties of a warrior from an entirely different perspective and, because of my newfound insight, was able to challenge the presuppositions I had held so dear. Eventually I developed the courage to question my self-deceptive cocoon, which had provided so much comfort to me. To my surprise, I began to see a path to increased personal effectiveness *and* improved tactical acumen. I learned that by consciously recognizing the humanity of the people with whom I dealt, I was subconsciously valuing their potential for dangerous levels of unpredictability. This awareness of their humanity allowed me to appreciate their adversarial worth.

I began to look more deeply at the warrior ethos I always thought I understood, and discovered what I now believe is the true nature of a warrior. A warrior is skilled in the combat arts; however, almost anyone can develop expertise in the various physical skills needed to fight by engaging in focused practice. One can undertake the physical activities associated with *warriorship* without understanding the nature of a warrior's character. The fiercest battle a warrior wages is an internal one. It is the battle against fears, biases, prejudices, and loyalties that prevent them from discerning right from wrong and acting for what is right. A warrior knows that the first step to being able to control others is becoming skilled at controlling oneself. There are many who battle outward influences and adversaries. However, the battle within *oneself* defines the warrior's path, and that battle is never-ending.

It requires an ever-evolving sense of humility to recognize this truth. This type of humility eluded me in my youth and, in all honesty, continues to elude me to this day. There is something attractive about seeing others as less important or less deserving. It provides a sense of security—albeit false security—that makes the world simple and easily understood. I labor to constantly study and reflect on the true warrior paradigm in order to honor the philosophy of unconditionally respecting *all* people I encounter. We must be careful not to confuse respect with friendship, admiration, or trust, all of which result from cultivating a personal relationship with another person over time. We can ill-afford to trust everyone we meet, but respecting him or her is a personal decision—a strict, tactical discipline. The way we choose to treat others, especially when we have options, has little to do with them, but instead speaks volumes about the content of our character. Our personal effectiveness and safety is dependent upon being able to be aware of, and responsive to, the reality of others.

Another thing I have come to realize during the course of my career is that this path is not for everyone. It falls to all warriors to make a consistent effort to invite others to embrace it, but be careful not to judge those among us who reject the invitation. The select few who choose daily to follow the warrior's path are obligated to model the philosophy in our daily lives and offer encouragement to those who pursue it alongside us. However, at the end of the day, we must remind ourselves to respect those who offer criticism of the warrior's way and reject it. Those who lack the discipline and desire to engage this way of life have much to teach us about ourselves, and we should listen intently to the message. For, like them, we too have weaknesses and, at times, lack warrior discipline. Their lack of commitment should serve to remind us of the times when we compromise our integrity and begin to serve ourselves, instead of serving others. With each success we enjoy comes the risk that we will come to see ourselves as having *arrived* at a place where we are better than those we serve. The truth is that our choices define our character and, in having chosen to serve, we have implicitly accepted that we may have to give our lives to save the meekest among us. There can be no greater way to honor humanity than by selflessly serving. I think that is what it means to walk the path of a warrior.

Charles "Chip" Huth is the President of the National Law Enforcement Training Center, a non-profit corporation dedicated to delivering effective training to law enforcement, security, and military personnel. Chip is a Sergeant with the Kansas City, Missouri, Police Department and has 19 years of law enforcement experience. He currently serves as a team leader for the Street Crimes Unit Tactical Enforcement Squad and has coordinated and executed over 1200 high-risk tactical operations. Chip is a certified national trainer in defensive tactics, an expert witness in the field of police operations and reasonable force, and a Subject Matter Expert on police use of force. He is an adjunct instructor at the Leadership Academy and a consultant for the KCPD's Office of General Counsel, the Missouri Peace Officers Standards and Training Commission, and the Missouri Attorney General's Office. He is a member of the International Law Enforcement Educators and Trainers Association and the National Tactical Officers Association, and is the President and CEO of CDH Consulting L.L.C., a law enforcement consulting and training company. Chip has 30 years of experience in the martial arts, with a background in competitive judo and kickboxing. Chip is the coauthor of "Unleashing the Power of Unconditional Respect-Transforming Law Enforcement and Police Training" (2010). He is a veteran of the United States Army and lives in Kansas City, Missouri, with his wife, Krista. Chip can be contacted at chuth@tacticalsolutionskc.com.

Things They Don't Tell You at the Academy

By James Dowle

I know how cops love hearing stories and anecdotes from trainers in order to better comprehend the learning points. I also know they like lists, bullet points and brevity, and can have a, "Yeah, yeah. Just give me the facts and cut the waffle"-attitude. So, with this in mind, I will attempt to suit both viewpoints and outline a few things I wish I'd known early in my police service. These are not tips on officer safety or law and procedure. These are designed to help you live through each day and ease some of the resistance that I have encountered over the years. In many cases, I have had to learn the hard way—often clashing heads with colleagues and supervisors when I thought I knew better. Sometimes I did, and other times I wished I'd kept my big mouth shut! I hope these points will save you hours of frustration, grief, and anger whilst doing a job you love. If you are starting out in one of the most stimulating and satisfying careers there is, I hope the lessons I learned the hard way may ease your path.

You are not Superman. Understand your physical, mental and, most importantly, your emotional limitations. Wearing a uniform and being depended upon by those in crisis can develop feelings of invulnerability and exceptional self-control. This makes it doubly hard to cope when you find you are no longer in control emotionally or when practical situations turn out badly. A personal example of this is from when I had about eight years service. I was the senior constable on a shift of about 25 officers in a busy city centre station. I was often relied upon by my sergeants in their absence to supervise younger officers.

One afternoon we had a call to a suspicious sudden death. It involved a thirty-something woman who was thirty-four weeks pregnant. She had collapsed at home after her routine health check and was found dead by her husband and two-year-old toddler when they returned to the house. By the time we were called, the body was in hospital and the baby had also died after a failed attempt by the doctors to save it with an emergency Caesarean. I knew that both my sergeants had young children and that one of them had actually lost an infant recently due to illness. I offered to take the call on their behalf and they were very grateful. I had no kids and wasn't married at the time so assumed I'd be unaffected. After all, I had my non-stick, trouble proof uniform on and I was at the top of my game. Suffice to say it didn't quite turn out like that. When I dealt with the dead mother and baby, it affected me very deeply. The deceased mother laying at peace in the hospital chapel looked serenely beautiful. It was difficult for me to accept as I looked at the distraught husband that his life and future had just collapsed around him. It seemed dreadfully unfair that such a hard-working, law-abiding guy had his world torn apart when the scum that I dealt with on a daily basis always seemed to get the breaks. The hardest part, however, was the thought that one day that guy could be me. I subconsciously decided that I would put up an emotional wall because I didn't ever want to let myself be that vulnerable. It was years before I would let anyone get close to me emotionally because I was terrified the same thing might happen. In fact, it wasn't until the trouble free birth of my own daughter years later that I think I finally laid that demon to rest. *If I knew then* about the cumulative effects of stresses on police officers through the work of people like Dr. Kevin Gilmartin and Trooper Bobby

Smith, I may not have carried that emotional baggage with me and allowed it to impact my personal relationships negatively for so many years. I implore you to research the lessons that the work of these men can teach you and put into practice the survival techniques they recommend, in order that you don't become the cold, hard, yet emotionally distant professional that I was for many years.

Be prepared to be limited by the inability of others. It's easy to want to forge ahead and create a "brave new world" of policing in your early years. Your natural enthusiasm and energy will often be abraded by others. These may be older colleagues, senior officers, or administrators. Accept early that not everyone shares your vision and abilities, but do not become cynical or angry. Search out ways to achieve your goals that do not trample on other's egos. This leads directly to the next point.

Be aware of egos, particularly your own. The police service is a traditionally masculine organization wherever in the world you happen to work. Today, thankfully, there are an increasing number of female chiefs, executive officers, and supervisors, but this does not totally dilute the masculine nature of most police organizations and the competitive egos within them. Police officers by the nature of their required character traits tend to be egotistical. Go on deny it! Look inside yourself and you will probably find there is an element of ego that goes with your choice of career and indeed your choice of career path within the organization. I am not presenting this factor as a negative thing as this *ego* comes from a pride in doing a job that we know many others could not and would not choose to do. It comes from the core tenets of standing up for the weak, not being willing to back down from conflict, and knowing that we serve the law itself and not some individual leader, politician or other person. It makes us feel good about who we are and what we do. Of course we have egos. Therein lays the problem. Unless you can manage the egos of your colleagues, supervisors and, most importantly, yourself, you could be heading for a boatload of grief. I'm not going to bore the reader with anecdotes about how many of these situations I've faced; instead, I'll (egotistically) offer some advice. The following points I've found to be true without exception.

- When a supervisor has a large ego, you will not succeed by challenging them. Find another way.
- Sometimes in order to succeed or bypass a problem individual, you have to temporarily swallow your principles, though never betray them.
- Occasionally it will help to be overheard by others to praise that problem individual, even if the words stick in your throat. All's fair in love and war!

This last point I have found to work particularly well in easing situations with supervisors that you have clashed with previously. There is no point getting angry about the situation, it will only harm you. *If I had known* this early in my service, it would have shaved years off my achievement of personal career goals.

Find a way to channel your anger. There are so many situations of unfairness, injustice, and intolerance in the world and we deal with most of them. You would have to be some kind of Buddhist religious guru to be unaffected by our work. That said, most officers tend to be able to cope quite well as they recognize that these things are part of the world in which we live. However, where officers do tend to allow the anger to spill over is when the injustice or unfairness comes from within the organization. It can eventually lead to the legendary police cynicism. I've wasted so much time over the years being angry with *them*, whoever *they* may be. This anger leads to victim orientated behavior and, let's face it, police officers never want to see themselves as victims. I have since found that being angry about a situation at work can never turn it around in my favor. It may give an ephemeral high as you curse the offending supervisor, administrator, lawyer, chief, politician, etc., and let off steam. Believe me, that's better than holding it inside; however, you need to channel that anger in more positive ways if you want a positive outcome. *If I knew then* that by taking an objective, emotionally neutral viewpoint (I know this is hard), I could have found a way through or around that particular problem, blockage, knock-back, change of policy, unwanted posting, or whatever it may have been that caused my anger. Accept that you are in a job that does not generally attract the best managers or leaders in the world. Add to that the fact that police organizations are generally politically controlled by those who rarely comprehend policing issues as well as the cop on the street, and it's natural that you will get angry. By channeling that anger in positive ways, I have learned to use that powerful energy to work towards where I want to be, rather than drowning in the negative emotions. Don't let them grind you down. Take a deep breath and work out where you want to be. Next, decide how you're going to make that happen and work hard. Unfortunately, that route will often involve relating with the very people that have caused you the anger. Accept now that if you want to get there, you will have to create a good relationship with those people and use them to help you get there. You can't do that if you're focusing all your energy on bad-mouthing them and resisting every direction you're given by them. You and your career are more important than the temporary feel good factor of letting off steam.

One person can make a difference. Remember why it is you became a police officer? It is easy as time goes by to be dragged down with negativity and the cynicism of others. The endless processes and procedures that seem to encroach daily on your ability to do the job can deflate the enthusiasm to make a difference and help people. In extreme circumstances, it can seem that the policies of the organization prevent you from doing what common sense, let alone everyone involved in the incident, dictates you should do to help. When working with other agencies outside the police, you will often find the optimum outcome is frustrated by their policies or by intransigent individuals who work within them. This is where you need to use your legendary powers of persuasion in order to achieve a positive outcome. At times like these, it is useful to remember your role and the oath you took when you joined. If you genuinely want to make a difference, you should work the angles and put in the effort. An extra 10 minutes work or effort on your part can change someone's life for the better. I learned the truth of this many years ago when dealing with a routine neighbor dispute.

I had been called to a social housing area where a complaint had been received from a female about the yobbish behavior of her neighbors. I was made aware that over 10 similar calls had been logged within the last month by the same complainant. On my arrival, it was all quiet and the incident was long over with no criminal behavior having been disclosed. How many calls have we all taken like this? It's easy to result the call as "all quiet, no police action required" and move on looking for more excitement. I used to do the same; however, on this occasion I was tired and took the opportunity to drink a cup of tea and actually listen to the complainant. She had three young children and had suffered a messy divorce. Her ex-husband had been wealthy but went bankrupt and she was left at the mercy of the local council to house her and her children. She had been put on a very undesirable estate and the council were aware of the social problems and the disorder, bullying, and abuse caused by the other residents. However, the housing department were dragging their heels in sorting out the problem. I looked at the kids and thought, "What chance will these nice kids have growing up here?" I left the address and drove straight to the council offices, and was seen without appointment. After only 15 minutes chatting to a housing officer, I left and got back to taking calls. All I needed to do was lend a little support to the mother's case by outlining all the previous complaints and the council agreed to prioritize her case and move the family. In all, that took me about an hour out of my day, a small investment, but for what reward? I received a letter about two months later from the mother who was very grateful. She took the time in the letter to write about how well her kids were doing again at school, how they were sleeping better at night and how she had now come off medication for nervous anxiety. She admitted that when I had attended her call she was approaching the end of the road and couldn't see a way out. Doesn't this result go to the core of the oaths we take as police officers? It's not as sexy as chasing and arresting robbers and rapists, but when I look back now over the "sexy arrests" I've made, not one of them leaves me feeling as satisfied as the difference I made to that young family. I'm not writing this to demonstrate what a "good chap" I am, but rather that one person can make a huge difference. All cops are privileged to hold it within their power to make these differences, and all cops will have similar stories. *If I knew then* that I could have such a positive effect on someone's chances for the future and quality of life, I could have helped so many more people. Don't underestimate the effect you can have for the better, as well as for the worse, on people's lives.

These are a few examples of lessons I've learned over the years. They are the lessons that the trainers at the academy don't teach you, but *if I knew then*, I'd have had a much more rewarding start to my police career.

Jim Dowle is a sergeant in Hertfordshire Constabulary, England. He has served for over 20 years, mainly in frontline uniform roles, and spent 11 years as a member of the Tactical Firearms Team, specializing as a sniper and close protection officer.

In 2003, Jim moved to the Force Training Department where he developed a unique Counter-Terrorism course that won the 2006 UK National Training Award. He is now a Judge and Ambassador for the UK awards. He has developed mental preparedness and emotional survival training in his Force, which is seen as a pioneer in the UK for these subjects. In 2008, he transferred to a role as training manager with a regional counter-terrorist unit.

Jim is also a Major in the British Army Reserve. In March 2009, he was mobilized to serve in Afghanistan where he was officer in charge of developing training and mentoring for Afghan Special Police Units. He is currently based in the UK in a staff role for the Ministry of Defense. He is working towards a PhD in Occupational Psychology through the University of Hertfordshire, to investigate the psychological impact of police sniper shootings and design appropriate training solutions. He also provides mental/attitudinal training for the Cambridge University Rowing Team.

Where Your Treasure Is, There Your Heart Will Be Also

By Travis Yates

As I write this, I have been a police officer for 17 years, 4 days. I was hired by the Tulsa (OK) Police Department when I was 21 years old and I literally blinked and here I write. My parents and veteran officers all told me the same thing: take your time, enjoy this job; it goes by all so very quickly.

Of course, like all 21 year olds, I did not believe them. They were so right. I have been blessed in my career. I've had, for the most part, the opportunity to do just about anything I've wanted to do. Yes, like most, I have had my problems with certain aspects of my agency, but I have vowed never to speak publicly about the Tulsa Police Department in a negative tone. I've had too good a time, in what others would call a job, to ever speak badly about the organization that gave me so many opportunities.

Today, I am looking downhill at my career and I am thinking about things I never thought I would. My last day as a police officer is getting closer each day and with that comes the thought of finances and security for my family. It is actually strange that I would think about family security and money. If I only knew then, what I know now, the thoughts in my head would be so much more peaceful.

I started as a police officer right out of college. While I had jobs before that, this was the first job I would consider a career. It was also the first time that I was living on my own and sustaining myself completely. There were no relatives in the city where I was living. Meaning, there wasn't a home-cooked meal to be had, anyone to do the laundry on weekends, and no one looking at my finances.

That last part is where the problem was 17 years ago and, because of that, where the problem in a sense remains. Now don't get me wrong. I'm not homeless or carrying around 25 credit cards, but the job as a police officer and the indoctrination that occurs early on is not always a positive thing when it comes to finances. Financial problems are not issues that happen overnight and they are not issues that get fixed overnight. The process is slow and gradual but, in the blink of an eye, you wake up and realize that you are in a mess.

The mess begins with the culture of the law enforcement world. Police officers love their toys and those toys go farther than guns, lights, and the other equipment that entire magazines show pictures of each month.

So, that is how it starts as a young officer, especially one that may have been living on pork and beans in college. You are getting a steady paycheck and you want to fit in. You love your job, you enjoy your coworkers, and you want what they have…toys! Those toys can take any shape. For some it is the bass boat—which, by the way, you can't take out on weekends because as the rookie you are working weekends. For others it's the safe full of guns—which, for most of them you can't carry on duty, plus you can only shoot one at a time anyway.

For me, it was cars. I loved them when I was 21 and I love them today. With these cars comes an incredible responsibility: monthly payments. Now, as a police officer, you can't exactly afford monthly payments on that new truck or Corvette but that is the beauty of being a police officer. There is no reason to worry about what the new toys cost because you can always work extra jobs.

Extra jobs to the typical new officer are like whiskey to an alcoholic. You can never get enough and eventually it will catch up to you. I've seen it over and over again, and despite my warnings to countless new officers, they always fall into the trap. There is a reason why a new officer will always find the extra jobs…the veteran officers have figured out they don't like to work them anymore. While extra jobs in themselves aren't inherently evil, the risk is great.

The extra jobs I liked 17 years ago, I now avoid like the plague. For many, the problem is that they use extra jobs to finance toys or, worse yet, their monthly lifestyle, and one of two things *will* occur. The extra job will go away, leaving a bill that can't be paid, or you will no longer want to work the extra job but you are forced to due to relying on the money.

It all comes down to time, and what any young officer finds out eventually is that your priorities will change. If they don't change, they should. For me it was about family. The time that I had to spend at the extra job paying for the toy, I would rather be with my wife, my newborn son, etc.

It is quite a dilemma and one I want you to realize sooner rather than later. There will come a time in your life where being a police officer is not the center of your entire world. It may be impossible to imagine as a 20-something-year-old, wearing a badge and a gun, but trust me, it will occur. The only thing that lasts in your life is your family. That must be your priority, and the one way you can show what your priority is will be the time you spend with them. If you don't believe me, look around. Do you know the guy that's on his third marriage and works as much overtime as he can? Do you know the officer that can't get to the bar quick enough after work but always complains about the problems he has with his kids?

Just as you have to make regular deposits of money into your checking account to pay for things, you have to invest time in your family for that to pay off. In a sense, I was the lucky one. I had a wife that put up with me working all the time and communicated to me, clearly, when she saw my priorities were mixed up. God sent us children who have turned my world upside-down and I want nothing more than to spend every waking moment with them. I missed a lot of years because I had to finish paying for my early mistakes in regards to finances and I may have to put off retirement a few more years because of those early mistakes. You will never get back the time you miss with your family when you are paying for temporary items here on earth.

In my limited experience, I have developed a few rules on finances. If I would have followed these rules 17 years ago, there is no doubt my life would be different.

- Limit Your Debt: A mortgage is the only debt permitted. If you think you can't buy a car or a toy without a payment, try following the rest of the rules and you will!
- Murphy: I hate this guy and he always comes at the wrong time. The easiest way to defeat him is to keep six months of your salary in the bank. When the car breaks down or the foundation of your house cracks, you can deal with it. If you follow this rule, Murphy may inconvenience you but he will not devastate you.

- The 10/10/10 rule: This rule is the key to success. Save 10% and you will soon get that "Murphy" resistance built up. Invest 10% and you will not have to work your entire life, and Give 10% to a charity that you care about. Trust me on that last one.
- Cash: You ever wonder why your grandparents knew how to manage their money? Credit cards didn't exist and they used cash. Even if you pay off your cards at the end of the month, research says you will spend more if you use a credit card over cash. Use cash at all times and if someone needs plastic, use a debit card.
- Home: There is no rush getting that first home. The tax benefits are not what they used to be, and Murphy always moves in with you. Owning a home is more expensive than renting. Start by renting a modest place and save the extra money. Take that extra money and use it for a large down payment. You will need it because you never want to finance a home longer than 15 years. Trust me on this one. If I followed this rule 17 years ago, I would now own my home!
- Extra Jobs: They aren't always a bad thing and we are blessed to have the opportunities, but never use the money for living expenses. Save that money and use it for your toys, a present or for your "Murphy" fund, because life will happen: you will need to replace a refrigerator or a car engine. Just trust me on this one!
- Raise: Occasionally this happens, and instead of immediately buying that boat or upgrading houses, try saving the extra money and throw it in an investment. I have a colleague that still lives on what he made 15 years ago and has invested the raises. Let me just say he is doing very well...*extremely*

well. When I am 50 driving to work everyday, he will be on a beach somewhere. You really need to trust me on this one!

In the most famous sermon given by the most famous preacher ever, Jesus Christ gives us a glimpse of where our treasure should be.

> "Do not lay up for yourselves treasures on earth, where moth and rust destroy and where thieves break in and steal, but lay up for yourselves treasures in heaven, where neither moth nor rust destroys and where thieves do not break in and steal. For where your treasure is, there your heart will be also." Matthew 6:19-21

I wish I knew then where my treasure and heart should have been. Many of you still have time.

Captain Travis Yates is a veteran of the Tulsa (OK) Police Department. He has a Master of Science Degree in Criminal Justice from Northeastern State University and is a graduate of the FBI National Academy. He is the owner of www.policedriving.com, a website dedicated to law enforcement driving issues, and he is the Director of Ten-Four Ministries, dedicated to providing practical and spiritual support to the law enforcement community. Travis was the 2008 Law Officer Magazine Trainer of the Year. He continues to work with agencies around the world regarding emergency vehicle driving issues.

The Witch Hunt

Guy Rossi

I thought I had the world by the balls. That was until our Chief of Police was arrested and the FBI started probing our special units. No matter what anyone says after the fact, personally witnessing men carrying machine guns walking into the Chief's office and removing him and his aide in handcuffs will leave an indelible mark on your psyche. Little did I realize that act would pave the road for all of his power-hungry subordinates to claw their way to the top. The chief, whom everyone had liked, unfortunately dipped his hands one too many times into the confidential informant funds for his own personal use.

As a result of the chief's arrest, a federal probe began that would be reminiscent of the Civil War, when brother was pitted against brother in a battle of ethics and ideology. The newly appointed chief was talked into having Internal Affairs partner up with the FBI investigation to probe for other corruption within the department. Normally, an officer under federal investigation is not obligated to cooperate with investigators when dealing with potentially self-incriminating matters. However, when they partnered with our internal affairs unit, officers had one choice: cooperate or face suspension for insubordination. On a personal note, this would have been okay if the powers that be only investigated the self-indulgences of the chief, but soon it would extend itself to investigating every public outcry of unlawful arrest and excessive force as well.

Just prior to the Chief's arrest, our agency had been very successful at creating a Street Crimes Interdiction Team, pairing narcotic and tactical investigators with street cops in plain clothes to address the growing number of homicides resultant from drug sales. The best officers from every precinct were assigned for a month or two and their job was solely to survey street-level drug sales and violence and immediately address violators with overwhelming manpower. For two consecutive years, this unit received mayoral awards for reducing street crimes and homicides to less than sixty percent of what they were in previous years. It was great. The law-abiding citizens were able to walk the neighborhoods again and cops felt like they were actually doing something proactive again.

All was fine until the drug dealers figured out how to exact revenge on those protecting society. It was actually a very simple strategy: complain to community leaders that the street enforcement teams were violating their constitutional rights by conspiring to steal from them and using excessive force when effecting arrests. In a heartbeat, over one hundred of the shining stars within our police department were dragged into interviews with Internal Affairs and the FBI. When it was all said and done, four officers were indicted out of over sixty that were considered. The latter faced the unthinkable; i.e., testifying against their peers or facing criminal charges, demotion, or being fired for not cooperating with an internal investigation. Officers faced charges of using excessive force in grey areas when they faced individuals who tried to draw weapons on them during search warrants, as well as allegations that cash and jewelry were stolen as the result of the arrests.

It would take nearly two years and a bevy of taxpayers' money before the witch-hunt ended and the four officers were exonerated. As a result, the spirit and backbone of the young up-and-coming officers was destroyed. It would be nearly ten years and many early retirements later before the department would begin to heal. Some people felt that airing our so-called "dirty laundry" in the courts and the media was the right thing to do. Did it restore public confidence in the department...maybe? I can tell you one thing: after the court case, no one returned to duty wanting to be proactive. Lessons learned: first, being part of an elite unit means you will eventually be scrutinized, if not by the public then by peers for reasons of power or jealously. Second, even the most popular of initiatives will be scrutinized when agency or governmental administrations change. Last, whenever we as pubic servants function in the grey areas and so close to the line between being proactive and the law, the legal system will endure longer than our willingness to split hairs over that which is politically correct.

Guy Rossi is a retired Police Sergeant of the Rochester, New York, Police Department who specialized in patrol, recruit, field training, and defensive tactics instruction. He has been a nationally recognized law enforcement trainer since 1982. His experiences in officer survival skills have been published in over two hundred magazine articles and chapters in books on training. Upon retiring from active duty, he was employed as a Program Coordinator of Curriculum Development for the Public Safety Training Facility of Monroe Community College (MCC). Presently he is a Program Coordinator of Curriculum Development for the Homeland Security Management Institute of MCC. Guy has a Master's Degree in Adult Education – Instructional Design. He is also a proud charter member of the International Law Enforcement and Educators Training Association (ILEETA) and serves as the Editor of the prestigious ILEETA Review. In his spare time, Guy continues to peck away at law enforcement training-related articles as well as a serial killer novel he has been working on entitled, "Bloodline."

Would I Have?

By Tim Harder

"If I knew then, what I know now"? If I had known in 1992 that I would be sitting at a laptop typing at 2:00 AM (sober, with two hours sleep and not being graded), would I have become a cop? Yes! If I knew then that I would have insomnia at least once or twice a week due to work, would I have become a cop? Yes! If I knew then what I know now about training the subconscious mind, would I have became a cop? Yes!

July 6, 1993. Six months on the job. I was working in a typical small-town Wisconsin police department. The kind of police department where you would get two or three calls for service a shift but would make 20 traffic stops to make your day go faster. It was 10:32 PM. In Wisconsin, 10-32 is the radio code for "man with a gun." Thinking back, was this a sign? I, along with the only other officer working in our police department, Mike, was dispatched to the adjoining jurisdiction for a man with a gun, ironically at 10:32 PM. Maybe that is why I remember the date, time, location, and events.

Of course, the jurisdiction we were mutually aiding and my jurisdiction were on two different radio frequencies. We had limited information or details about what was going on without the ability to communicate until the dispatch centers patched up their radio systems. Finally, we were told a white male had come into his estranged girlfriend's workplace with a gun. The suspect had shot the manager and was attempting to locate his ex-girlfriend.

With four days of field training and six months on my own, I didn't know all the streets in my own jurisdiction, let alone the ones five miles away. I was headed there, lights and siren on, with a rough idea of the location. Lucky for me, the incident was taking place on a main road where I bought groceries. It seemed like it took me a half hour to cover that five miles. Limited traffic, no real traffic obstructions, just thinking, "What the hell am I going to do when I get there?" As I say, I knew what street the call was on, but I had no idea of the building or block numbers. I made it to the street wondering how to find a building number in the dark without driving right up on the call. Finally, the dispatcher gave me a cross street. Holy shit! I was about 100 yards south of that cross street. I pulled into the first available driveway and killed my lights and siren. As soon as the siren stopped, I could hear gunshots. I didn't know if they were shooting at me, or if it was the suspect or the cops doing the shooting. What I did realize is that my training had already kicked in. Not the geography training of knowing where I was at all times, but my tactics training. I had exited the squad car and knelt down behind the engine block near the front tire.

As I heard a second and then a third gunshot, a voice came over the radio. "8535, shots fired." That was the officer's call sign from the adjoining jurisdiction. As the transmission stopped, I heard car tires squealing. That would not be last time I heard those car tires squealing that night.

I looked north of my location to the noise of the squealing tires and saw a dark vehicle accelerating at a high rate of speed just two driveways from my location. "8535 the suspect is leaving southbound in a dark sedan," the officer yelled into the radio. Again, training took over. I went to get back into my squad car to pursue but I couldn't get my door open. Not because it was broken or because I locked the keys in it (like most rookies), but because I had my gun in my hand. When I initially got out of my squad car and heard the gunshots, I pulled my gun and knelt down behind the engine block, just like in training.

I quickly re-holstered my gun and the pursuit was on. The pursuit lasted all of about four *straight* blocks. If I knew then that hitting a large electric pole, head-on, would hurt and total a squad car, I may have been grateful for only four straight blocks, but that is another story. The four blocks seemed like everything was in slow motion. As we entered block two, I observed the suspect swerving. Not a little swerve, but one of those good, drunk driver swerves. The car looked like a pinball, bouncing from one curbside to the other. Later, I surmised that the swerve was caused when the suspect tried to retrieve his shotgun from between the passenger door and the seat.

As we neared the end of block four, I saw that we were approaching a T-intersection. The suspect went left and I followed behind him. Obviously, the suspect didn't know the streets either. A left turn immediately displayed a "Dead End" sign. Upon seeing the sign, the suspect took a hard right into the first business driveway. Again, my tactics training kicked in. Is this a set up? I didn't know the area or location to tell the dispatcher. I created more distance between the fleeing vehicle and me. As the car continued behind the building, I cautiously followed.

I saw the suspect had driven through the yard, some shrubbery, and then exited on the opposite side of the business. Being a probationary officer, I didn't want to damage one of my department's only two squad cars. I backed-up the way I came in.

When I reached the street, I heard my co-worker, Mike, call out that the vehicle was coming right at him. When I got to the other side of the business, I saw the fleeing vehicle as it slammed into the driver's side of Mike's squad car…and I was concerned about a little grass and shrubs damaging the squad car. As I got out of my squad, not knowing if Mike was inside of his, I heard that sound again. The squealing tires. The suspect had lodged his car on the rear bumper of Mike's squad. Now he was accelerating back and forth in an attempt to dislodge from the squad. The acceleration increased. It looked like a drag strip. With the tires heated up so much, the air had filled with smoke and the smell of burning rubber.

I began about a 50-yard sprint. Again, I had my gun in my hand before I knew it. As I got about 15 yards from the suspect's car, I heard gunfire. Mike and three other officers had to rely on their training that night. The suspect died from a gunshot wound to the head.

Mike and I approached the driver's side of the vehicle with the tires still squealing, with smoke filling the air, due to the suspect's weight pushing on the accelerator. We secured him and were able to stop the squealing tires.

If I knew then what I know now about how the subconscious mind works, would I have became a cop? Yes. The subconscious mind can store many, many memories and images. This early career event was a positive memory as it showed me that I could rely on my mind to revert to my training and experience in the time of need. If I knew then, what I know now about training the mind, I would have kept a detailed daily journal to refresh my memory.

There are good memories established by scenario training, imagery, and life experience. Giving your job the best effort and keeping a positive attitude will lead to a happy, lengthy career. The difficult memories may lay dormant for an eternity; however, those that surface may do so when you least expect it. They can be triggered by a smell, a sound, or a war story.

I tell new officers early on in the academy, from the training you receive and the life experiences you will have in law enforcement, you will never be the same person again. It is how you view them both that will shape your career.

Tim Harder is a Training Officer for the City of Madison, WI Police Department. He has 14 years of experience with the Madison, WI Police Department and four years with the McFarland, WI Police Department. His professional assignments have been as a Neighborhood Officer, Educational Resource Officer, Patrol Officer, and S.W.A.T member. He holds a Bachelor of Science degree from the University of Cincinnati and Masters of Science degree from the University of Wisconsin-Whitewater.

Your Life IS Your Legacy

By Brian Willis

When I started my law enforcement career in 1979, the last thing on my mind was the question, "What legacy am I creating through the way I live my life?" For the first six months, I was just focused on working hard and doing the best job I could in basic training. Once that task was accomplished, my next point of focus was working hard in the field to be accepted by "the real cops out on the street." I knew that police work was a brotherhood and that it was important to be accepted and trusted by my fellow officers.

This second part got off to a rocky start. It was made abundantly clear to me that my first field-training officer, the first partner I was ever assigned to work with, hated rookies. His disdain for rookies was compounded by the fact that he had to give up a partner he really liked working with when he was ordered to work with me. For my first week, we were assigned to late car night shift in our patrol district. As the "late car," you started thirty minutes after all the rest of the night shift cars and ended the shift thirty minutes after they went home.

Working the late car sucked.

The *suck* of working the late car was compounded when my FTO refused to talk to me for the entire first week. We spent every night that week driving around in absolute silence unless there was a reason he had to talk to me. I was determined to stay focused, work hard, and slowly I began to develop a reputation as a good young cop (still with a lot to learn), and I developed a bond with my partner. By the end of our six weeks together, we got along great and continued to be friends.

The next 25 years seemed to fly by with a series of new challenges: getting through my field training phase, getting off probation, getting married, becoming a father, getting transferred to a new district, becoming a father again, finally getting into the tactical team after four attempts, getting promoted and transferred to a new district, learning to be a supervisor, blowing out my right knee, being assigned from an operational position as a supervisor to an administrative position while recovering from reconstructive knee surgery, becoming the NCO in charge of training and development for our Crowd Control Section, learning to be a soccer coach, learning to be a cub leader, obtaining a sergeant position in the Training Section, learning to be a basketball and football coach, taking over as the supervisor in charge of the officer safety, use of force, EVOC and incident command programs, serving as Deputy Commander of the Crowd Control Section during the World Petroleum Congress and the G8 Summit...and finally...preparing for and accepting retirement.

Each of those challenges was a tremendous opportunity for me to learn, mature, and grow. However, if you were to ask me during most of my 25 years as a police officer about the meaning of a legacy, I likely would have thought about things we leave behind when we die, or structures like the speed skating oval and bobsleigh track in Calgary that are often referred to as legacies of the 1988 Winter Olympics.

It was not until late in my career when I was asked to put together a presentation for a police officer retreat on the concept of "your legacy" that I began to reflect on this topic.

As I explored this topic, I began to understand that a legacy is not something we leave behind when we die; rather, it is something we create every day that we live. I have since spoken and written about the concept that *your life IS your legacy* to officers around North America.

Each of us has many roles in our lives. Those roles include:
- Mother/father,
- Son/daughter,
- Sister/brother,
- Husband/wife,
- Warrior,
- Professional,
- Partner,
- Leader,
- Coach,
- Mentor,
- Learner,
- Teacher,
- Friend.

In each of those roles, we interact with a variety of people, creating powerful and lasting legacies every day. These legacies are the result of our day-to-day interactions, our daily actions or inaction, and how we respond to difficulty and tragedy. Not all of these legacies, however, will be positive.

What will help us to ensure that we are creating the most desirable legacies throughout our lives is life's most powerful question: *What's Important Now?* If we can accept that our life is our legacy and embrace this question early in our lives, it will have a profound impact on our words, our actions, our relationships, and our accomplishments.

In retrospect, I think I did okay in most of those roles over the past 30 years. However, if I knew then what I know now and had embraced the concept that *your life IS your legacy* earlier in my life, I could have done better than okay. I could have done a better job as a father, husband, law enforcement professional, supervisor, warrior, and leader.

I encourage you to take the time to reflect on your life and the legacies that you create in each of the roles you live every day.

Brian Willis is an internationally recognized thought leader, speaker, and trainer. He draws upon his 25 years of law enforcement experience as a member of the Calgary Police Service and 20 years of training experience to provide cutting-edge training to law enforcement officers and trainers throughout North America. Brian operates the innovative training company Winning Mind Training, and is the editor of the highly acclaimed books "W.I.N.: Critical Issues in Training and Leading Warriors" (2008), "W.I.N. 2 Insights Into Training and Leading Warriors"(2009), and "If I Knew Then: Life Lessons From Cops on the Street" (2010); www.warriorspiritbooks.com. Brian serves as the Deputy Executive Director for ILEETA and is a member of NTOA, ITOA, IALEFI, and the Canadian Association of Professional Speakers. Brian can be reached through his website at www.winningmindtraining.com.